LOPER LEGACY

BUILDING A WINNING CULTURE AT NEBRASKA-KEARNEY

BY CRAIG SESKER

LOPER LEGACY
Building A Winning Culture
At Nebraska-Kearney

By Craig Sesker

Copyright: 2024 Marc Bauer, Dalton Jensen, Nebraska-Kearney
Wrestling
Edited by Jennifer Lowery
Foreword by Kurt Karjalainen
Photos: Marc Bauer, Nebraska-Kearney
Cover design by Ben Strandberg
Published by Kingery Printing
Designed by Angie Hardenbrook
Cost: $25.00

Printed in the United States of America

First Edition

FOREWORD

By Kurt Karjalainen
UNK All-American, 2000 NCAA finalist

Times were tough in the world of college wrestling from the 1970s through the 1990s. Top decision-makers at NCAA to NAIA programs across the country played a pivotal role in deciding the future of wrestling at colleges. The popular norm quickly became cutting wrestling programs from their university systems.

College programs took a significant downward turn, losing 462 programs from 1972 to the end of 1997.

When I landed at the University of Nebraska at Kearney in 1997 to wrestle for the Lopers, it is safe to say UNK was not known as a national powerhouse. Nor was it as prestigious as it is now in the wrestling community. After our 1998 season ended, I vividly remember walking downstairs in UNK's Heath & Sports Center between classes to a very small office shared by head coach Jeff Cardwell and assistant coach Marc Bauer. I recall leaning against the wall while I listened to Cardwell recite his planned conversation before leaving for a meeting with the athletic director. Coach had written four pages, prepped with notes that listed the program's successes from our year. Smiling ear-to-ear, Coach Cardwell stood up from his desk and followed with a lighthearted laugh before saying, "Wish me luck!"

Coach Cardwell was excited when he left his office. It wasn't even 20 minutes later when he returned looking chin-whipped by his opponent. He looked defeated as he shuffled back in the room. Cardwell reported the athletic director had no intentions of hearing the list of achievements, plans to grow, or the ideas he had outlined on paper. It was the complete opposite.

Pretty quickly, I read the room and realized that these two coaches needed to talk without a student wrestler's ears overhearing. I left with trepidation about my future and the future of the UNK wrestling program. But I knew deep down these two would figure out a way to power through this adversity like any wrestler would do.

Without the full support of all university personnel, UNK wrestling was up against a tough road for survival. Little did I know exactly what fire that set off in Coach Bauer over the next year. After the following wrestling season, Coach Cardwell left the program and Marc Bauer became head coach in 1999. Over the next 17 years, everyone learned that Coach Bauer had a visionary mindset that elevated the UNK wrestling program to what it is today. With an unbelievable work ethic, Bauer built the foundation for what became nationally known as a powerhouse program.

A program that has produced national champions, Academic All-Americans, and hard-working, smart, tough, resilient men who lead classrooms, businesses, households, and give back to their communities.

To this day, under the direction of head coach Dalton Jensen – by independent fundraising, alumni backing, and the UNK support – the wrestling program continues to build strong men. These men lead by examples of the past and foster relationships in the present. UNK wrestlers know they are part of something special.

I look forward to reading and remembering stories about the individuals who came together against all odds to build a Legacy that is Loper Wrestling.

CHAPTER 1
PAVING THE WAY

Brian Hagan didn't have to travel far to attend college. He grew up in Gibbon, Nebraska, a town of 1,200 people located just outside of Kearney. Before he joined the University of Nebraska at Kearney wrestling program, Hagan had an outstanding high school career.

He was a two-time Nebraska state champion for Gibbon High School in 1984 and 1985. He placed third at state as a freshman and finished second as a senior in 1986. He competed at 105 pounds his first three years before bumping up a class to 112 as a senior.

Hagan had drawn the attention of college recruiters, and although he eventually chose UNK, he had initially intended to attend another school.

"I was pretty much signed, sealed and delivered to go to Nebraska-Omaha," he said. "Then Ed Scantling, the head coach at Kearney, called and said let's go out for lunch. He twisted my arm and persuaded me to go to college in Kearney. My girlfriend was already at UNK and I decided to go there."

5

Hagan landed a spot in the starting lineup at 118 pounds for the first meet of his freshman year and stayed there for his entire four-year career with the Lopers.

Hagan qualified for the NAIA national tournament as a freshman and sophomore in 1987 and 1988. But he fell one match short of becoming an All-American both years.

"It was frustrating and disappointing," he said. "But it kind of lit a fight under me. I wasn't used to not placing in big tournaments. Getting so close and not sealing the deal, it made me work harder. Coach Scantling kept talking to me and encouraging me."

Scantling had a significant impact on Hagan.

"Coach Scantling was really good at relating to people," Hagan said. "And he could put things in perspective. He was calm, confident and collected. He was really good at motivating you. We had some tough practices. He pushed you to be the best you can be."

Hagan received his third opportunity at the NAIA nationals in 1989 in Jamestown, North Dakota.

"I wrestled in the very first match of the tournament and I got upset in the first round by two points," he said. "I was pretty upset. Scantling found me outside and tried to calm me down. He told me that 'the sun is going to come up tomorrow. Get out there and compete and do your best.' I got on a roll after that.

"I ended up wrestling the same kid that beat me in the first round and I ended up beating him 9-1 in the match for fifth place. I finished fifth and got on the podium. That was a big step for me."

Hagan came back his senior year convinced he could

achieve a goal he had set when he started college.

"My sights were set on winning the national title," he said. "It was my last chance. And I knew I could do it."

Hagan was on track to reach his goal until a setback late in the season.

"I was wrestling pretty well until about three weeks before nationals," he said. "I threw a kid with a lateral drop and I hurt my back. I had to sit out for two weeks. I went to the doctor and the trainers worked on it. About a week before nationals, I came back and started training. It was still bothering me when we got to the national tournament."

Hagan was the No. 1 seed at 118 pounds for the 1990 NAIA national tournament on March 1-3 in Hays, Kansas. He was in a full 32-man bracket and would have to win five straight matches to capture the championship.

Hagan opened with a pair of lopsided victories. He downed Eric Lewis of Huron 10-0 before rolling past Shannon Long of Findlay by a 23-7 technical fall. Then it became challenging.

Hagan battled a familiar foe in the quarterfinals in Dennis Friedland of Adams State. Hagan had won two previous matches against Friedland, with one victory by just two points. This match would be close as well with Hagan pulling out a 9-7 win.

"He kind of hung back and was able to keep the score close," Hagan said. "But I was able to push through and advance."

Hagan thought he might have his hands full in the semifinals. And he did. His opponent, Kirt Allen of

Alaska Pacific, had placed third at nationals the year before. Plus, Allen had defeated Hagan in a previous meeting.

But not this time. Hagan won one of the best matches of the entire tournament, outlasting Allen 15-14.

"It was a barnburner," Hagan said. "He slammed me and knocked me out. They were thinking of stopping the match. But I took my injury time and was able to continue wrestling. It was a really tough match.

"I was relieved to come out of there with a win. It was like wrestling a twin. He was just like I was – he was short and stocky and in great shape. It was a battle."

Hagan had advanced to the finals. And his final collegiate match would be in the national championship match.

"I was excited to be in the finals," he said. "I knew my teammate Ali (Amiri-Eliasi) was going to win it. He had demolished everybody. I didn't want him to be the only one celebrating."

Before that could happen, Hagan had to get past a tough foe in Steve Meuer of Western Montana. Meuer had placed at 126 the year before and then dropped down to 118.

"He was tall and lanky," Hagan said. "It was a totally different matchup. It was another tough match."

The match was tied 4-4 after regulation and went into overtime. Hagan held a 5-4 lead in the closing seconds of overtime and was defending on his feet. Hagan, who had not been warned for stalling during the match, was called for fleeing the mat. The officials gave Meuer a point and the wrestlers ended the overtime period tied 5-5.

The match would be decided on criteria. Hagan and Meuer stood together on the center of the mat as the referee went to the scorer's table.

The referee then walked to the center of the mat and raised one of the wrestlers' hands. It was Hagan's.

"It went to criteria. And it came down to the first reversal, which I had," Hagan said.

Hagan had become the first national champion in Loper wrestling history.

"I tried my first ever backflip on the middle of the mat," he said. "I got three quarters of the way over. I landed on my feet and fell forward on my hands and knees."

Hagan stood up and had a huge smile on his face.

"I was super excited," he said. "It was crazy. A dream had been reached. A lot of work went into it. Becoming a national champion, that was my goal when I started college. To finally reach that goal was pretty unbelievable."

Hagan's mind was racing during the medal ceremony.

"Standing on top of the podium, I was so appreciative of my coaches and teammates for pushing me and helping me," he said. "It was all kind of surreal. It was quite an honor to be the first wrestler from our school to win a national title."

Roughly an hour later, the Lopers had their second national champion when Amiri-Eliasi won the national title at 150 pounds.

"Ali was a great wrestler," Hagan said. "He was stocky and he was strong. And he was really good technically. He was always in control of the match. He made it look easy at times. Watching him motivated and inspired me."

Hagan finished his collegiate career as a two-time All-American at Nebraska-Kearney. He compiled a 96-33-1 career mark, including a 29-4 record his senior year. He was named to the Lopers' Team of the Decade for both the 1980s and the 1990s.

Hagan stayed involved with the sport for decades after graduating from college. He worked as a full-time teacher and coach before retiring in 2023.

He was the head coach at his alma mater in Gibbon for five years before teaching middle school science and physical education in Kearney for many years.

He coached middle school wrestling for 15 years and started the Kearney Mat Cat kids wrestling program. He also served as an assistant coach at Kearney High under UNK alum Ty Swarm for 10 years.

Hagan and his wife, Hallie, who also is from Gibbon, have been married for 34 years. Hallie is also a teacher. They have two adult children.

Their daughter, Hattie, lives in Billings, Montana. She recently gave birth to a son.

Their son, Brogan, lives in Columbus, Ohio.

Brian Hagan, who turned 56 in 2024, is a member of the Nebraska-Kearney Athletic Hall of Fame, the UNK Loper Wrestling Hall of Fame and the Nebraska Scholastic Wrestling Coaches Association Hall of Fame.

Hagan still follows the Lopers closely during the winter months.

"It's been amazing to see what has happened with the UNK wrestling program since I competed there," Hagan said. "Marc Bauer and Dalton Jensen have done an incredible job running the program. The success they have had is phenomenal. It's really been impressive to see.

"They also have done a great job of really keeping the alumni involved with the wrestling program. When they say it is a family atmosphere, it really is. I am very proud to be a part of the UNK wrestling family."

CHAPTER 2
FROM IRAN TO UNK

Alireza Amiri-Eliasi's story is remarkable. The path he followed to become a two-time national champion at Nebraska-Kearney is quite fascinating. And almost unimaginable.

Amiri-Eliasi was born in Iran on February 20, 1962. He grew up in Kermanshah in the western part of the country.

"It is an area that definitely loves its wrestling," he said. "They love wrestling in Iran – it is their national sport. They have a huge appreciation for the sport and are very passionate about it.

"That is why Jordan Burroughs and David Taylor, Americans who won Olympic gold medals in wrestling, are considered legends in Iran. The Iranians appreciate and admire their greatness."

Amiri-Eliasi was 13 years old when he was introduced to the sport of wrestling in Iran.

"They had a youth program and someone told me about it," he said. "I wanted to give it a try. I went to only three or four practices, and then they sent me to my first tournament. I entered the city championship and I won. But then I went to the state championship and I got spanked. I got beat by a lot of points in one match and got pinned in another."

After that first exposure to wrestling, he was hooked.

"The following year, in 1976, I won the state title and I won the national title in Iran," he said. "They had one division from 8 to 16 years old. I was 14 years old and I won the 50-kilogram national title. That was a really big deal. I qualified to compete in an event in America."

Amiri-Eliasi then went to a training camp in Tehran, Iran before flying to the United States to compete in the youth world championships in Minneapolis, Minnesota. He finished second, falling to an American wrestler in the finals.

"It was a good experience," he said. "I found a sport I was passionate about. I loved the process of training and competing. I followed what my coaches told me – they were great technicians who taught me a lot. I developed a strong work ethic. I knew this is what I wanted to do."

Two years later, Amiri-Eliasi won state and nationals again in Iran. He earned another trip to the United States, traveling to the U.S. Olympic Training Center in Colorado Springs. And he captured a gold medal at the 1978 high school world championships at 57 kilograms.

"It was an amazing moment," he said. "I was representing Iran. They had a medal ceremony and they played the Iranian national anthem. It was a very important moment. It was one of the biggest achievements in my life. It still gives me goosebumps when I think about it.

"I was doing really well and I was on track to achieve some bigger goals that I had in wrestling."

A year later, in 1979, everything changed for Amiri-Eliasi. The Islamic Revolution started in Iran. And a war began between Iran and neighboring Iraq.

Amiri-Eliasi had just graduated from high school, and his wrestling dreams were put on hold.

"The war started and I got drafted into the Iranian Army," he said. "I spent two years in the Army. I was actively involved as a soldier in the war for 21 months. I was stationed at the Iranian-Iraqi border.

"I had no opportunity to wrestle during that time. I worked out when I could to stay in shape, but I was unable to train for wrestling or compete."

Amiri-Eliasi operated a machine gun and he traveled to the front of the war zone. He would look for enemy soldiers from Iraq. When he discovered their location, he would radio it back to camp.

"And then they would send bullets and attack the enemy in the location I gave them," he said. "I saw a lot of bloodshed. I saw a lot of young people get killed on both sides. It was pretty traumatic. It definitely bothered me. I had too many friends that were killed in the war. I spent 18 months at the front, right where the war was going on.

"It was very scary. At some point in life, you get kind of numb to it all. It was very surreal. When you see too many people torn apart, it takes a toll on you. Over a million people died in that war. It was a bad period in history."

Amiri-Eliasi returned to competition after serving two years in the Iranian Army. He made a strong return to the mat. He won Senior Nationals in Iran in 1983 before finishing second at the prestigious Yasar Dogu tournament in Turkey.

"I lost to a South Korean who was third in the Worlds," Amiri-Eliasi said. "I got head-butted in the semifinals and got a concussion. I won that match and then I tried to wrestle in the finals. But after 30 seconds my coach stopped the match.

"I wasn't able to keep going. I had really bad swelling above my right eye. And I definitely had a concussion although they didn't really diagnose those like they do now."

Amiri-Eliasi was back on the mat in Iran, but not for long. He opposed the new leadership in his home country, and the Islamic regime didn't take kindly to people who did that.

"One of my friends got executed at age 16 because he was selling a newspaper they didn't like," Amiri-Eliasi said. "I was worried the same thing might happen to me because of my views. I decided I needed to leave. If I wouldn't have gone, I could have been executed or jailed. Plus, I am Kurdish. I was a minority, and I wasn't important to the new rulers in the country."

Amiri-Eliasi said he paid a person for a visa so he could leave Iran for Pakistan.

"We weren't supposed to leave the country, but I had to get out of there," he said. "There was a lot of corruption. I decided to leave right before Christmas in 1984. It was a bad situation."

Amiri-Eliasi left numerous family and friends behind in Iran.

"I had six brothers and two sisters," he said. "My dad passed away when I was a soldier. My mom and my siblings were all still in Iran when I left. They knew I was planning to leave because I wasn't safe.

"I went to Pakistan, then East Germany and then Sweden and back to East Germany and then West Berlin. It was a couple of months in each place. When I was in Sweden, they said I was illegal and they wanted to send me back to Iran. That is why I went to East Berlin and West Berlin. I applied to be a refugee and it was accepted."

He landed in a refugee camp in West Berlin for a couple of months. He was sent to Ingelheim, Germany, a city located just west of Frankfurt.

"I was fearing for my safety and for my life," Amiri-Eliasi said. "I just wanted to survive. I knew it would better where I was. When I got to the refugee camp, there were people there from a lot of different countries. We played soccer and we would wrestle around for exercise."

In 1986, a janitor at the camp saw Amiri-Eliasi wrestling and told him that there was a wrestling league he could possibly join.

"I worked out and one of the coaches – Coach Muller – asked me to practice and wrestle with their team," Amiri-Eliasi said. "I was a refugee, but the coach got the paperwork done so I could join their team. I was able to go there and wrestle. They had a room for me to live in and they provided my meals. The government took care of it. We were in Mainz, Germany. They signed me up for a language class to learn German."

Amiri-Eliasi wrestled freestyle for the team from Mainz in a league in Germany.

"I had a record of 125-1 at 68 kilograms," he said. "The only match I lost was up a weight class. It was a great experience to be back competing again."

In 1987, Coach Muller took Amiri-Eliasi and a group of wrestlers to the U.S. as part of an exchange program with Nebraska.

"I wrestled in Omaha, Kearney and Ogallala," Amiri-Eliasi said. "I wrestled against college Division I kids and beat most of them. I was 25 years old at the time. I wrestled in Kearney and was with Tom McCann, who was one of the coaches. He asked me, 'Do you want to come here and go to school?'"

Two years later, Amiri-Eliasi decided to accept the offer.

"Ed Scantling was the head coach for UNK and Tom McCann connected us," Amiri-Eliasi said. "I was 27 years old. I told them I wanted to coach. I thought I was too old to wrestle, but they asked me if I wanted to wrestle for them."

Coming to America was a major transition for Amiri-Eliasi.

"When I came to Kearney, I spoke Farsi, Kurdish and German and a little bit of English," he said. "After I came there, I was always studying English. I was either working out or studying when I was in college. I got my bachelor's degree and master's degree when I was at Nebraska-Kearney from 1989-95. I had a 3.5 grade-point average. Wrestling opened the door for me. I needed a college degree to coach."

Amiri-Eliasi also embarked on one of the best wrestling careers in Nebraska-Kearney history. He won the NAIA national championship as a freshman at 150 pounds in 1990 and captured the NCAA Division II championship at 150 pounds in 1991.

"I worked really hard and had good coaches and teammates who pushed me," he said.

Amiri-Eliasi nearly won a third straight national title in 1992.

"I made it back to the finals," he said. "But I lost in overtime and took second. We were wrestling at altitude in Colorado and it was tiring."

Amiri-Eliasi came back and became a four-time All-American as a 31-year-old senior for the Lopers in 1993.

"I ruptured my pectoral muscle early in the season at the Omaha Open," he said. "I was out for two months. Coach Scantling said, 'You are done wrestling.' But I ended up coming back with one arm and got third in Division II that year."

It wasn't quite the finish he had envisioned, but Amiri-Eliasi still had a remarkable college career.

"I had an opportunity to wrestle in college in the United States, and that was amazing," he said. "I was very well disciplined. I had goals I wanted to accomplish in wrestling and beyond wrestling.

"I was very focused on studying and training.

"I never went to parties. I wanted to stay focused and take advantage of my opportunity."

Amiri-Eliasi's achievements led to his induction into the NCAA Division II Wrestling Hall of Fame and the Nebraska-Kearney Athletic Hall of Fame.

"I have very fond memories of my time in Kearney," he said. "Coach Scantling changed my life. He gave me an opportunity to come to Kearney and an opportunity to be able to afford it. I got an opportunity to come to the United States. Not many people have an opportunity like this. I had to take advantage of it and make the best of it.

"I was a person who was not afraid to take risks. If I wouldn't have left Iran, I might have been executed. It wasn't easy to leave a place I grew up in. I have good friends in Iran that I am still in contact with. But I knew I had to leave Iran at that time to have a better life."

After Amiri-Eliasi graduated from UNK, he landed his first full-time job in the U.S. He was hired full-time by the Boys and Girls Club in Amarillo, Texas in 1995.

He had previously worked as a camp clinician in Amarillo during the summers when he was in college. Among the wrestlers he worked with was Brandon Slay, who went on to win a gold medal at the Olympics.

"They contacted me and asked me to go coach and work with kids," he said. "I worked there for three years from 1995-98. I was the physical education director and wrestling coach."

From there, Amiri-Eliasi taught and coached wrestling at River Road High School in Amarillo from 1998-2001.

He also continued to compete. Amiri-Eliasi fought 22 times in mixed martial arts, compiling a 20-2 record. He also was coaching grappling.

Following two years in Kissimmee, Florida, he ultimately ended up on the East Coast. Amiri-Eliasi accepted a position in 2005 as a teacher and coach at Bullis School, an independent college preparatory school in Potomac, Maryland. He has been there ever since.

Amiri-Eliasi has two sons, Sepanta and Soshiant, who are both excelling in wrestling.

"My sons are both very coachable," he said. "And they are passionate about wrestling."

Amiri-Eliasi is a proud man who became a United States citizen in 1992.

"I came to America for a better opportunity and for freedom. And to have a better life," he said. "When I became a U.S. citizen, it was one of the best and proudest days of my life. Coming to America has opened so many doors for me."

Amiri-Eliasi continues to make an impact in a sport he has been involved with for half a century.

"Wrestling is such a great sport," he said. "It gives you discipline. It builds you for life. What you learn from it – the work ethic – it builds character. It isn't easy. It's tough and demanding, but it's rewarding. Wrestling saved my life. I really truly believe that. Who knows where I would be without it? I took a risk to leave Iran, and I'm not regretting what I did. Wrestling helped me in so many aspects of my life."

Amiri-Eliasi also keeps close tabs on his alma mater.

"I still follow the wrestling program at UNK," he said. "Marc Bauer went in there and did a great job as the head coach. They have been very successful. Marc did a very good job there."

Amiri-Eliasi has fond memories of his college days at Nebraska-Kearney.

"I am fortunate to have had the chance to go to school and wrestle there," he said. "I am proud to be a part of the program's history at Kearney. Without Kearney and Coach Scantling, I wouldn't have everything that I have in my life now. That was a really pivotal and important time in my life. I am so incredibly grateful that I had that opportunity in Kearney, Nebraska."

CHAPTER 3
MAKING HIS MARC

Marc Bauer grew up in Kearney. He excelled as a high school wrestler under Hall of Fame coach Tom McCann at Kearney High School.

Following his prep career, Bauer had an opportunity to wrestle for another Hall of Famer. University of Nebraska at Omaha coach Mike Denney offered Bauer an opportunity to wrestle for the Mavericks and he accepted.

"I was very fortunate and blessed to learn from two outstanding coaches," Bauer said. "They not only were great coaches, but great people who really cared about their athletes."

Bauer was an All-American for UNO from 1991-93, placing seventh, sixth and third at the NCAA Division II Championships. He was a member of Denney's first NCAA championship team in 1991.

Following his collegiate career, Bauer planned to pursue a teaching career.

"I had gotten a student teaching placement at Boys Town," he said. "My original intent was we were going to stay in Omaha. Then I received an opportunity to teach in Kearney. My wife got a job at Good Samaritan Hospital.

And I was teaching fourth grade.

"I didn't really have a desire to get into coaching. But the first thing that happened when I came back to Kearney was Tom McCann wanting me to coach at Kearney High. I also had an opportunity to coach middle school wrestling."

Bauer's starting salary as a teacher at the Kearney schools was $19,900. He received another $3,000 to coach.

"For me, it was a nice sum of money to coach," he said. "My brother, Joshua, was going to be on the junior high team. He was going into seventh grade. That team had David Miller, Frank Kuchera, Lance Tolstedt and Joshua Bauer. That team went on to win the only state title in Kearney High School history."

Marc Bauer's services were in high demand in the wrestling community. He also received an opportunity to coach at the collegiate level.

"Jeff Cardwell was the head coach at UNK," Bauer said. "He asked me if I would like to coach at Nebraska-Kearney. They offered me $5,000. I was going to coach junior high kids as well. I coached junior high for a couple of years and I enjoyed that. But I really fell in love with coaching the kids at the college level. We had some success."

Bauer was an assistant coach when Nebraska-Kearney finished second in the Rocky Mountain Athletic Conference Tournament in 1999.

"We qualified seven wrestlers for nationals, but we had six guys that went 0-2," Bauer said. "Andy Sistek won a match. But then he threw his headgear and lost a team point, so we actually finished with zero points.

"After the season, we were going into spring break. I got back home from nationals and Jeff resigned. Jeff recommended me as the next head coach. Mike Sumpter was the athletic director and he made his pitch.

"Jeff said you can do the job," Sumpter told Bauer. "And if you want it, it's yours."

Bauer had taken a new job as an elementary physical education teacher. Before he could take over the UNK program, he needed permission to leave school early two or three times a week because of his coaching obligations.

"The Kearney Public Schools were totally on board with me doing that," Bauer said. "I did that for 14 years and it worked out great."

Bauer was 29 years old when he became the interim head wrestling coach at the University of Nebraska at Kearney in 1999. A short time later, Sumpter was relieved of his duties as athletic director. And there was talk that UNK might be dropping some athletic programs.

Bauer had put together a feasibility study and wanted to show how much money the wrestling program was bringing into the athletic department.

Bauer was hired as the head coach at UNK for an annual salary of $30,000. Cardwell, his predecessor, had been making $45,000.

"We had a pretty small budget," Bauer said. "We got $26,000 in scholarships. After my first year, we were cut down to $14,000. Then it was cut down to $10,000. I'm not sure all of the reasons, but UNK brought in a lot of new coaches that were younger and could be paid less.

"The athletic department wasn't in good shape at all. It seemed like every head coaches' meeting we had was like doom and gloom. They were all about budget and budget cuts. It was frustrating."

Bauer wanted to ensure that the wrestling program had the financial support it needed to be successful.

"I received permission to try and raise money for our program," he said. "We started having camps and tournaments. We started a summer league. We had fundraisers. We found ways to start making money to help our wrestling program. Quite frankly, if we hadn't done that we wouldn't be where we are today."

It didn't take long for the program to start thriving again.

"We went from last at the national tournament in 1999 to eighth in 2000," Bauer said of his first season as head coach. "We had the same seven wrestlers and they qualified again. It was at South Dakota State. I was named Amateur Wrestling News Rookie Coach of the Year."

The Lopers then took a step back, finishing 23rd at nationals in 2001. But as Bauer said, "It eventually just took off."

Making the fundraising easier was that Bauer and the UNK wrestling program started having success early in his tenure. The Lopers finished second at the 2003 national tournament.

Senior Frank Kuchera led the way, capturing a national title for the Lopers at 174 pounds. Brandon

Pfizenmaier placed second at 149 and Bryce Abbey took third at 125. Three UNK wrestlers – Adam Keiswetter (133), Riley Ross (165) and Jeff Sylvester (197) – finished seventh at nationals.

Nebraska-Kearney later landed wrestlers who went on to become among the best athletes in the world in their respective sports.

Heavyweight wrestler Tervel Dlagnev won two NCAA titles at UNK in 2007 and 2008 before becoming a standout with USA Wrestling. He became an Olympic bronze medalist and a World bronze medalist.

Kamaru Usman won an NCAA title in 2010 before going on to win a title belt in the Ultimate Fighting Championships.

Romero Cotton became the first Loper to capture three NCAA championships from 2014-16.

Bauer coached the Lopers to NCAA Division II team titles in 2008, 2012 and 2013.

A program that was in danger of being eliminated is thriving with Bauer now serving as UNK athletic director and Dalton Jensen serving as head coach.

The Lopers also took a big step forward after they moved into a new wrestling room in December 2022. The wrestling program raised nearly $2 million to make the practice facility become a reality.

The generous support of Ron and Pam Blessing provided the biggest boost.

"Ron became a very close friend," Bauer said. "He was a UNK booster who started supporting wrestling. Blessing Construction is a company that he owned in

Kearney. We were talking one time and Ron told me they had left something in their will for the wrestling program.

"I told him we could turn the swimming pool into a new wrestling room. He talked to his wife. A week later, he decided they wanted to support that. They agreed. A big portion of the money came from Ron and Pam Blessing. We went to our administrators and said we had over $1 million for the project. They have absolutely been a blessing for us."

Unfortunately, Ron Blessing was unable to witness the completion of the sparkling new wrestling facility. He was involved in a construction accident and was killed a week before the 2022 national tournament.

"It was an absolutely horrible, horrible ordeal," Bauer said. "It was a really sad situation. Ron and Pam were great supporters of our program. We are so grateful for the contributions and the money they pledged for the wrestling room."

The Ron and Pam Blessing Wrestling Facility opened to rave reviews. And it offers many of the amenities that Bauer and Jensen had envisioned for the Loper program.

"It has 5,500 square feet just for wrestling with three full-sized mats," Bauer said. "There is also room in there for weight equipment and cardio equipment. We have our own athletic training room. Athletes have their own locker room and coaches have their own locker room. There are separate offices for the head coach and the assistant coach. This definitely shows the support the program has garnered over the years."

Many of the alumni have remained supportive of the program. Usman came in for a banquet that raised over $200,000.

The project had a few challenges along the way, but those were overcome.

"I am just ecstatic about this facility," Bauer said. "It's taken a lot of great people along the way to get to this point. I helped orchestrate and direct some of it, but it took a lot of people to make this happen."

One of the people who played a significant role in the Loper wrestling success was Ty Swarm, who was an All-American at Nebraska-Kearney during Bauer's first season as head coach in 2000.

Swarm completed his eligibility a year later and was hired by Bauer as a UNK assistant coach. Swarm served in that role until 2013 when he became the head wrestling coach at Kearney High School. He went on to become an assistant principal at Kearney High.

"Ty was definitely a big part of the success we had in wrestling at UNK," Bauer said. "He was with me as an assistant coach for 12 years and we made a great team. We balanced each other really well. He's more analytical and more of a manager than I am. He really helped build our plan for a lot of fundraising.

"Ty was great at building relationships with our athletes. He definitely made a big difference for us in a lot of ways. We wouldn't have had the success we did without him."

The program has come a long way since Bauer first became head coach.

"I just played the hand I was dealt," he said. "I had some good kids who really bought into what we were doing. The program is in very good hands with Dalton being the head coach now. I got to coach Dalton Jensen for two years, and then he was my assistant."

Bauer has made a seamless transition from coach to administrator at Nebraska-Kearney.

"I absolutely love the athletic director job," he said. "I love the challenge. It's been really rewarding. I know what the coaches are going through and that is a huge advantage for me. The connections I have in the community, that helps a great deal as well.

"I taught 18 years in the Kearney Public Schools. That gave me an opportunity to interact and connect with a lot of people in the community through their kids."

Bauer and his wife, Beth, raised their four children in Kearney. They have two sons, Ryan and Scott, and two daughters, Allison and Julia.

Ryan Bauer wrestled for his father at Nebraska-Kearney while backing up national champion Daniel DeShazer. Ryan Bauer delivered a big win that was pivotal in a dual meet victory over rival Chadron State.

There have been so many special memories for Bauer during his tenure at the University of Nebraska at Kearney.

"Kearney is such a great community and I've been blessed to spend my entire career here," he said. "It's such an amazing place."

CHAPTER 4
PERSISTENCE PAYS OFF

Frank Kuchera grew up in the wide-open spaces on his family's ranch in Rose, an unincorporated community in north central Nebraska. Kuchera excelled in wrestling at a young age. He qualified for the state tournament during his freshman and sophomore seasons for Rock County High School.

Competing in Class D, Kuchera went 1-2 at state at 126 pounds as a freshman in 1995. The following year, Kuchera won his first match at state at 135 pounds before dropping his next two.

Following his sophomore year, Kuchera decided to make a move.

"I had developed some ties at Kearney through wrestling," he said. "I have an older sister, Peggy, who was living in Kearney and I moved there for my junior year of high school."

Kuchera enrolled at Kearney High School and was looking forward to wrestling for one of the state's top programs under head coach Tom McCann.

Before joining the wrestling team for the winter

season, Kuchera decided to go out for football at his new school. Midway through the 1996 fall season, disaster struck for the 140-pound Kuchera. Kearney High was playing at rival North Platte.

"I was on defense and there was a big pileup," he said. "The play was over and as I was getting off the pile, I was down on one knee. Then I got knocked backwards. I landed on my back. And my football cleats were in my armpit. It was my right foot and right leg, and it wasn't good.

"I don't remember too much pain until they put me on a stretcher and straightened my leg.

"I had broken my femur. It twisted it in half. I ended up having surgery in North Platte. I was in the hospital for 10 days and I was in a wheelchair for a few weeks. I still have a 10-inch scar on the right side of my leg from that injury."

The injury in football meant Kuchera likely was going to miss his junior season of wrestling.

"I was a new kid in a new school, and I had broken my leg in my first semester at Kearney High," Kuchera said.

Kuchera already knew a number of wrestlers on the Kearney team. And he began his long road back to becoming healthy again.

"It obviously was disappointing to have that happen," Kuchera said. "But my teammates on the wrestling team were supportive. And Coach McCann and Coach (Dennis) Miller made sure I didn't get too discouraged."

Within four months, Kuchera had started to work out and drill toward the end of the wrestling season.

"I was kind of hoping to be back before districts," he said. "But my knee wasn't feeling quite right."

Kuchera went in for an MRI on his knee and doctors discovered he had also torn the anterior cruciate ligament in his right knee when he was injured playing football.

"I had another surgery, and I essentially started from scratch again," he said. "All of my rehab was similar. It was frustrating, but I was determined to get back 100 percent. That was the one and only focus. I wanted to get back on track so I could wrestle my senior season."

Kuchera had ACL surgery in March of 1997 and wasn't cleared by doctors until late in the summer. One thing was certain – he wasn't going out for football as a senior.

All of his focus was on achieving his goal of winning a state wrestling championship.

"I was full go when school started – I was good to go," Kuchera said. "I had to wear the big clunky ACL knee brace. I didn't have any setbacks after that and I wrestled a full season."

Kuchera was part of a loaded Kearney High team that went on to capture the Class A state championship. Senior David Miller led the way, earning his third individual state title.

"That season was a blast," he said. "We had a phenomenal team. We had an incredible amount of talent on that state championship team. David Miller was amazing. He had a great career."

Kuchera was on course to achieve his goals. He entered the 1998 state tournament ranked No. 1 and he was unbeaten on the season. Kuchera powered into the 160-pound semifinals after pinning his first two opponents at the state tournament at the Devaney Center in Lincoln.

Kuchera was set to face Lincoln East's Matt Wheeler, a wrestler he had defeated earlier in the season, in Friday night's semifinal round. But the rematch turned out differently. Wheeler posted a 5-2 upset over Kuchera.

"I am sure he made some adjustments, but I couldn't get it going," Kuchera said. "I was completely drained afterwards. I had some anxiety and nerves that affected me.

"It was a defining moment for me. I couldn't really sleep that night because I was so upset about that match." Kuchera regrouped with a pin in his next match en route to a third-place finish in his final state tournament. He had finished his career with a victory like he had hoped.

"I bounced back the next day," Kuchera said. "It was bittersweet. We ran away with the team title, and it was great to be a part of it. But I was disappointed that I didn't win a state title."

Kearney had five wrestlers in the finals with Miller and heavyweight Lance Tolstedt winning individual state titles.

"We had a heck of a team, that's for sure," Kuchera said. "We had a great season and we had some really good wrestlers on that team."

Kuchera's dream had been to wrestle for the

University of Nebraska. His brother, Chad, had walked on and wrestled for the Huskers for a couple of seasons.

"But I didn't have much of a track record," Kuchera said. "I didn't have very many schools interested in me."

But one college did eventually reach out.

"Coach McCann put in a good word for me at UNK, and they showed some interest," Kuchera said. "I took a visit and I liked it there. And it looked like I had a chance to wrestle right away.

"I didn't really talk to any other schools. But UNK offered me a scholarship and I accepted."

Kuchera graduated from Kearney High School in 1998 before enrolling at the University of Nebraska at Kearney the following fall.

He landed a spot in the UNK starting lineup at 174 pounds as a true freshman for the 1998-99 season.

"It was tough, going from high school to college. It was the next level and it was a big step up," Kuchera said. "I finished 15-15 my first season. I had a few bright spots, but I definitely took a few lumps. I also had a chip on my shoulder. I had a lot to prove. One of my goals was to be a state champ in high school. When that didn't happen, it motivated me to want to do well in college."

Kuchera's progression continued the following season at 174. He qualified for the 2000 NCAA Division II Championships in Brookings, South Dakota. He went 0-2 at nationals but showed considerable improvement from his freshman season.

"I knew it was going to be a process for me," Kuchera said. "I was trying to improve each year. We won our regional and the team was getting better. Kurt Karjalainen made the finals for us. I remember sitting and watching Kurt with my teammates and thinking 'this is really cool. That could be us.' I was thinking that it could be me.

"When I started college, my goal was to be a national champion. After my first two seasons, that was still my goal and I felt like I was progressing toward that."

Kuchera had been recruited to UNK by Jeff Cardwell before Marc Bauer took over as the program's head coach the following season.

The Lopers were also progressing as a team and finished eighth in the nation in Bauer's first season as head coach in 2000.

"Coach Bauer is a smart guy and a hard worker," Kuchera said. "He's very good with people and knows how to get the most out of his athletes. He did a great job building that program."

Kuchera's goals were put on hold at the start of the 2000-01 season. He suffered a torn right labrum at Dakota Wesleyan to start the season. He underwent surgery and was able to take a redshirt that season. Kuchera still had two years of eligibility left.

"I felt like it was part of the plan," he said. "I did my rehab and supported the team. The shoulder surgery was one of the worst that I had. It was the most painful initially. I had to sleep in a recliner for the first week or two. It was a long road back after that injury."

Kuchera came back strong the following season at 174 pounds for the 2001-02 school year.

"Our team was coming together," he said. "A few of us had redshirted. Everybody was back in the lineup. We were starting to be competitive with Nebraska-Omaha. Our goal was always to beat them."

The Lopers finally broke through to defeat their Nebraska neighbors to the east. UNO was a powerhouse program under Mike Denney. Bauer knew the program well, having been an All-American for the Mavericks on a team that won a national title.

The teams met late in the season with UNK knocking off UNO in a dual meet held in Kearney.

"Beating UNO, that was the greatest thing ever," Kuchera said. "That was one of our main goals. It was a big step for the program."

Kuchera also was taking more steps forward with his own wrestling. He had been nationally ranked at 174 before finishing second in the conference tournament.

Kuchera opened the 2002 national tournament in Parkside, Wisconsin with a first-round victory. Then he ran into Jon Duncombe of St. Cloud State in the quarterfinal round.

"It was tied late in the match. There was sweat on the mat and I stepped in it and slipped and the guy got a takedown," Kuchera said. "We were in a scramble and it was an unfortunate situation where I slipped. He won the match in regulation.

"It was heartbreaking, but I had to get ready for my next match right away to be an All-American. I was confident and I won my next match. It was a great feeling to become an All-American for the first time."

Kuchera moved on to face Augustana's Tom Meester, who had been upset in the semifinals. He lost to Meester before coming back to finish fifth.

"After the tournament, I don't remember being too disappointed," Kuchera said. "The season was such a grind. I became an All-American for the first time and I had won my last match of the season. And we had finished fifth as a team. It was a pretty good finish.

"And now I was in position to make a run as a senior. This was all a part of the process. I thought I had as good a shot as anybody to win a national title."

Kuchera also knew it wasn't going to be easy. Meester and Duncombe, the two wrestlers he lost to at nationals, were both returning. And so was Nebraska-Omaha's Bobby Edmonds, who had finished second at the 2002 NCAA meet. Edmonds started the season ranked No. 1 as the top returning wrestler at 174.

Kuchera started the season ranked No. 4 nationally and wrestled up a weight class at 184 pounds in the first two tournaments.

Kuchera passed one of his first big tests of the season when he met Edmonds at the UNK Open and emerged victorious.

"That was a good win for me," Kuchera said. "Bobby was ranked No. 1 at the time."

Kuchera's next big test came at the National Duals. He faced Meester and lost 7-3.

"He was a really good wrestler and he took me down twice," Kuchera said. "Meester was ranked No. 1 after that."

The Lopers went on to win the National Duals while knocking off Nebraska-Omaha again.

"That was a fantastic day for us, winning that event at Ohio State," Kuchera said. "Winning the National Duals, that was another landmark win for us."

Kuchera was still wrestling well in a loaded weight class. But then he had an unexpected setback in the final home dual meet against Fort Hays State.

"I lost in overtime," he said. "It was embarrassing. I was supposed to be a leader and one of the best wrestlers on the team. That loss definitely motivated me. It brought me back and refocused me."

Kuchera never lost again. He won the conference tournament and was part of a UNK team expected to contend for its first national team title.

Kuchera's conference title earned him his third trip to the national tournament. And then he received unexpected news. Meester didn't qualify for nationals. He had been ill and had to pull out of the North Central Conference Tournament.

"Meester was the only guy I hadn't beaten," Kuchera said. "I felt like the weight class was wide open for nationals. I definitely had an opportunity to win a national title."

Kuchera entered the 2003 NCAA DII tournament in Wheeling, West Virginia as one of the favorites. He won his first match by fall, but the next three matches were going to be difficult.

Kuchera downed Thad Pike of North Dakota State 4-1 in the quarterfinals. He then earned a clutch 3-1 win over Zach Stephens of SIU-Edwardsville.

"Stephens was really big and strong," Kuchera said. "I got a go-behind from a front headlock for a takedown to win 3-1."

Pike went on to finish third at nationals and Stephens took fourth.

Kuchera had advanced to the finals against a familiar foe. He would face Duncombe, who had defeated him in the national quarterfinals the previous season.

The nerves and anxiety Kuchera had battled in his final state tournament weren't there in his final college tournament.

"I was in the zone and I felt great," he said. "I slept great during that tournament. I felt supremely confident. I felt like it was my tournament to win. I had put the work in. I felt like it was meant to be. I didn't know how exactly I was going to do it. But I felt confident."

Kuchera came out strong in the finals, hitting a high crotch to score the first takedown. Duncombe then escaped and the first period ended with a 2-1 score.

The rest of the match was fairly uneventful. The wrestlers traded escapes in the second period before Kuchera earned a 3-2 victory.

"I knew my defense was good enough," he said. "I felt like nobody could score on me."

Time ran out and Kuchera raised both arms in the air. He had captured a national championship.

"I waved to my family and to our fans," he said. "I ran over to the corner and gave Coach Bauer and Coach Swarm a hug. It was an amazing feeling – it was so surreal. It was something I had worked for my whole career. When it happened, it was very special. It was a special time."

Kuchera led the Lopers to a second-place finish in the team race.

"We had a great team that year," he said. "It really helps when the other guys on the team are winning. We feed off that, and it really helps motivate each other."

Kuchera used that setback in high school to help him achieve his college dream.

"Not winning state really pushed me to get to that point," he said. "I felt like I wanted to and needed to prove myself."

Kuchera became the third national champion in school history and the first under Bauer.

"It had been a few years since UNK had a national champion," he said. "It was an honor to be Bauer's first champion."

Kuchera graduated from Nebraska-Kearney with a major in sports communication and a minor in sports administration.

He continued to stay involved with the UNK program. He was a volunteer assistant coach on the 2008 Loper team that won the school's first national championship.

"That was a total team effort," he said. "That was pretty amazing. To see it finally come to fruition, it was a cool experience."

Kuchera has continued to stay involved in the sport. He serves as the color commentator for the state wrestling broadcasts each February on NETV.

He still lives in Kearney and works in orthopedic medical sales. Kuchera and his wife, Amy, have three children. He has two daughters, Darby and Audrey, and a son, Henry. All three compete in wrestling along with various other activities.

Kuchera is a member of the NCAA Division II Wrestling Hall of Fame and the Nebraska-Kearney Athletic Hall of Fame. Not bad for someone who did not win a state title.

"Wrestling for Nebraska-Kearney, it was a fantastic opportunity and a great experience for me," he said. "I am super proud to have been a part of it. To see where the program has gone has been great. I couldn't be more proud of that program.

"We have that family dynamic with the wrestling program at UNK. It really is a family atmosphere – it is 100 percent true. We had a really solid core of guys and I am so fortunate I had the opportunity to be a part of that program. I wouldn't trade that experience I had at Nebraska-Kearney for anything."

CHAPTER 5
BIG MAN ON CAMPUS

T ervel Dlagnev was born in Bulgaria and spent the first three years of his life there. But conditions were far from ideal for Dlagnev and his family. And the country was dealing with its share of turmoil and political unrest.

"We were poor and my parents were looking for a better life for us," Tervel said. "We wanted the American dream."

Dlagnev's parents, Ivaylo and Igrena, made the difficult decision to leave Bulgaria. They informed Tervel and his older sister, Krassimira, what they had planned to do.

The Dlagnevs prepared to leave Bulgaria for a refugee camp in Austria. The family was packed and ready to go. They had planned to leave the country by train the following morning.

"But my mom had this feeling that we needed to leave that night and not wait until the next morning," Tervel said. "My parents talked about it and ultimately decided we needed to go that night. We got on a train that evening and we left Bulgaria. At 2 a.m., they closed the border. If we hadn't left when we did, my life would be significantly different.

"We left around 9 p.m. Thank God my mom wanted to go that night. She felt incredibly uneasy about waiting until the next morning. That turned out to be an incredibly wise decision on her part."

The Dlagnevs then moved to the refugee camp in Austria.

"There was one apartment building in the middle of a big grassy field," Tervel said. "There were a bunch of families there and a lot of them were from Germany. We were there for a year. I was almost fluent in German by the time we left. I also taught myself how to ride a bike when we were in Austria."

After a year in Austria, Dlagnev's father obtained green cards that permitted the family to move to the United States. They were coming to America.

Tervel was 4 years old when he stepped foot on U.S. soil for the first time. The Dlagnevs settled in San Diego, California and his father joined the United States Army. He was stationed in San Diego.

The Dlagnevs lived in an apartment in San Diego. Tervel and his sister, who is two years older than he is, were enrolled in English as a Second Language classes.

"I didn't speak any English when I came to the United States," Tervel said. "I struggled with the language. My sister was doing really well, and progressing and advancing. But I was having a tougher time learning the language.

"I was getting frustrated. It turns out that my sister is just brilliant. She is very intelligent and she loved school. She went on to earn a bunch of degrees. She has amazing comprehension – it is off the charts. She would read six books and I would read three chapters from one book. It turns out that I was pretty normal for my age. She was just really advanced for her age. She now teaches AP engineering at a high school."

After completing first grade in San Diego, Tervel moved with his family to El Paso, Texas.

"I was still learning English, and I got put in a regular second grade class and it was way above my level," he said. "I had never done the pledge of allegiance before. They started doing it and I had no idea what to do. The teacher we had, she yelled at me to put my hand on my heart. I put my left hand on my heart before she corrected me. I pretended to say the words because I didn't know them.

"Then the teacher had us going around class and was having everyone read the words from something. I was trying to sound out the words like I did from my ESL classes in California. Then the teacher said to me, 'Are you dumb? Do you need to go to bilingual class?' I went home crying that day and said I didn't want to go to school anymore."

The next day, Dlagnev was enrolled in a bilingual class. And everything started to change. For the better.

"I will never forget my teacher, Miss Navar. She taught my bilingual class from second grade through fifth grade. She was great," Dlagnev said. "She was very compassionate and she was very patient with me. She got me excited to try and read. The first book I read from cover to cover was in her class. She was incredibly positive. She really cared about the students. That teacher made an incredible impact on me."

Dlagnev was learning, but still struggling with self-esteem.

"I had very little confidence, and I wasn't involved at all in athletics. I was kind of shy and wasn't involved in much of anything in terms of school activities," he said. "My dad was in the Army and was away from home a lot of the time. Then he drove a truck and was away from home. My mom was a janitor and worked 18 hours a day. We were just trying to survive as a family. We didn't have much money. We were living paycheck to paycheck as my parents continued to adapt to being in a new country.

"I never remember being hungry. I do remember my mom having a $5 bill and she said that was for the next few days until your dad gets his paycheck. My parents were very stressed financially."

After a few years in El Paso, the Dlagnevs moved to the Dallas suburb of Arlington.

"I started out at Duff Elementary in Arlington, Texas," Tervel said. "At that point, I went into the regular classroom. I was ready. I wasn't really super traumatized because I had made good progress with my English in El Paso. I was in an apartment complex, and I made some friends from the students that went to Duff with me. I felt a little more comfortable."

Dlagnev made friends, but he was "running around

with a rougher crowd."

"I remember I was at a friend's house and we were jumping on the trampoline," Dlagnev said. "A guy knocked on the door and my buddy, who was a sixth grader, gave this adult a bag of weed.

"Later on, the police came in and handcuffed this kid and took him out of school. My friend was running drugs as a sixth grader."

Dlagnev said that "there were drugs around me everywhere."

"People were smoking pot around me," he said. "The parents were smoking bongs while we played video games in the next room. I never did any drugs. I refused when they asked if I wanted any drugs, and they didn't pressure me after that. I was their friend and they respected my decision."

During his early years in Arlington, Dlagnev rollerbladed, skateboarded and rode BMX bikes.

"One time, I tried to jump these stairs and busted the rim on my bike," he said. "It cost $80 to repair it and my parents couldn't afford to fix it."

In seventh, eighth and ninth grade, Dlagnev's passion shifted to Pokemon.

"It was the first generation of Pokemon cards, and I got really into that," he said. "I went to tournaments. I had competitive decks. It was my thing. I loved it."

As Dlagnev became older, his interest shifted from Pokemon into other areas. His collection of cards was stored in his family's home. Until they found another home.

"My parents moved and my mom got rid of the Pokemon cards," he said. "I wish I would've saved them. I had every card. They would've been worth a lot of money. My collection would've been worth close to a million dollars if I would have kept them. A lot of the cards were worth thousands and tens of thousands of dollars. I kept the cards in cases and they were in good condition. At the time she got rid of them, they didn't have the value they do today. I obviously wish we would've known that when my mom got rid of them."

Dlagnev had never played a sport, but that changed during his sophomore year in high school. He decided he wanted to join the wrestling team at Arlington High School.

"The main reason I went out for the team is that I wanted to get in shape," he said. "And I wanted to meet some girls. I figured if I lost weight and got in better shape and looked better that I would be able to meet more girls."

Henry Harmony, the wrestling coach at Arlington High School, had asked Dlagnev if he wanted to come out for wrestling.

"I probably weighed about 215 pounds, and I went on a crash diet and started working out," he said. "I dropped down to 165 pounds. I was around 5-foot-11 or 6-foot at the time. I didn't really like wrestling at first, but I liked the fact that I was getting in shape and losing weight."

Dlagnev wasn't able to compete in any meets during his sophomore season for Arlington High.

"I was failing my classes so I couldn't compete – I was ineligible because of my grades," he said. "I went to every single practice and did all the training. But I didn't wrestle any matches."

The summer between his sophomore and junior years of high school was pivotal for Dlagnev. Coach Harmony had asked him to compete in spring and summer wrestling tournaments.

"That's when I fell in love with the sport," he said. "I started eating healthier and I learned how to diet."

That carried over into Dlagnev's junior season at Arlington High.

"I got my grades up and became more disciplined," he said. "I wrestled at 180 pounds. My first match that season, I pinned a kid that had teched me just a few months before. I pinned him in the rematch because I had improved that much over the summer."

Wrestling was a good fit for Dlagnev because he moved well for someone in a heavier weight class. The mental aspect was the most difficult part of the sport for Dlagnev.

"I had never competed in anything," he said. "My anxiety was really high for competitions. I was really nervous before every match. I thought I was going to lose before every match. I would pin a kid and then think I was going to lose if we wrestled again. It was crazy, but that was how my mind was working."

Once he stepped on the mat and the whistle blew to start a match, Dlagnev would settle in and be able to compete.

"I was strong, fast and athletic for my size," he said. "I was diving at guys' ankles. The low single was what I wanted to do. I had watched a lot of videos of (Olympic and World champion) John Smith. He shot a lot of low singles for takedowns and that's what I liked to do."

Dlagnev was a quick study. And he had a successful junior season.

"As the season progressed, I started building my confidence," he said.

Dlagnev finished 48-7 as a junior and placed fourth at the Texas state tournament.

"Going to state, there was a lot of anxiety," he said. "But I got in there and scrapped and beat a couple good kids. I lost in the semis. I got thrown on my back in the consolation semis and came back to win in overtime. And then I lost in the third-place match."

Dlagnev moved up to 215 for his senior season. He weighed around 210 and didn't have to drop any weight that season. Dlagnev went 45-3 with 43 pins as a prep senior.

He entered his second Texas state tournament in 2003. He advanced to the semifinals when he ran into a wrestler from El Paso named Shawn Jordan.

It was a back-and-forth bout. Dlagnev scored two takedowns and held a 4-2 lead late in regulation. But Jordan scored a reversal to send the match into overtime. Dlagnev shot in on a leg attack during OT, but Jordan countered and spun behind him for the winning takedown.

"He was very athletic and super strong," Dlagnev

said. "I was obviously really bummed. I beat myself up. It was disappointing but not devastating."

Dlagnev came back to finish third. Jordan, who went on to play fullback for a national championship football team at LSU before fighting in the UFC, went on to win the state title that year.

Dlagnev had finished fourth and third at the Texas state tournament, but he wasn't drawing much interest from college recruiters.

One school that was interested in Dlagnev was the University of Nebraska at Kearney. Andrew Bauer, an assistant at Arlington High, was the brother of UNK head coach Marc Bauer.

"My brother called me and said he had a wrestler who had placed high in Texas," Marc Bauer said. "He said he weighed about 205 pounds and was pretty quick. He said he was a skateboarder who collected Pokemon cards."

Dlagnev, who also could have gone the junior college route, visited Nebraska-Kearney. He wanted to attend a four-year college and earn his degree from there.

"Kearney offered me $600 for the first year – that didn't even cover the cost of my books," he said. "But I figured I could take out student loans. So I went to Kearney. My visit wasn't great. I was super shy, and they took me to a party and I didn't drink.

"The coaches were nice and they wanted me to wrestle for them. I didn't really have any other options. It was a good opportunity to wrestle in college and I was like, 'Let's do it.'"

Dlagnev had committed to UNK and he was determined to take advantage of his opportunity.

"I was super committed to be successful. I have OCD (obsessive-compulsive disorder). A lot of my family is like that," he said. "I never got diagnosed, but my obsession became to be perfect at wrestling. That is what I was focused on.

"Coach Bauer asked me, 'What are your goals?' My response was that, 'I want to be a national champion.' He probably didn't think this $600 walk-on was going to win a national title. But I believed it and that was what I was shooting for."

Dlagnev was part of an excellent recruiting class at UNK that included future Loper All-Americans Joe Ellenberger and Jeff Rutledge.

"I connected with Jeff and Joe right away," he said. "I had never been away from home and it was tough at first. Once we started team activities and we had a retreat, that is when the team really connected. That is when I started to fit in. I wasn't super social. I needed some structure and I had that with the wrestling program."

Dlagnev started his collegiate career wrestling in the 184-pound weight class.

"I was a bad weight cutter. I made weight three times and then I broke my foot," he said. "I was wrestling a kid from Wartburg College and I rolled my ankle. It was at the Lone Star Duals in Texas in January 2004. It kept hurting, and I got an X-ray and it was fine. Then I was warming up for a dual and it rolled again. The MRI showed two broken bones in my right ankle."

Dlagnev was granted a medical redshirt by the NCAA and still had four years of college eligibility left after being injured.

Following the 2003-04 season, Bauer sat down and talked to Dlagnev.

"I remember Coach Bauer telling me to be super disciplined," Dlagnev said. "He wanted me to shrink my body and make 184 again. We had a national champion, Jeff Sylvester, in our lineup at 197. When I first went there, I didn't score a point on Sylvester the first semester in practice."

Instead of trying to make 184 again, Dlagnev decided to do something different.

"I went home for a couple weeks after the school year and bought every weight gaining supplement I could find," Dlagnev said. "I went back to Kearney and was weighing 215 pounds. I said, 'Coach, I don't know what happened.' That's when I became a heavyweight."

Dlagnev competed at his new weight class at the Cornhusker State Games over the summer and then he won a wrestle-off against the returning starter. He would start his redshirt freshman season as the Loper starter at heavyweight during the 2004-05 school year.

Dlagnev had grown to 6-foot-2 and was weighing between 215 and 220 pounds during his freshman season. He eventually climbed to No. 2 in the NCAA Division II rankings.

"I adapted really well at heavyweight," he said. "I could get to the low legs. I shot a lot of low singles. I wrestled pretty well."

During that season, he met a wrestler named Les Sigman from Nebraska-Omaha for the first time. Sigman, a junior, was a two-time national champion.

"I wrestled Les at the UNK Open and he beat me 9-4," he said. "I did take him down late in the match. He was trying to major me and everyone was freaking out after I took him down. Sigman was really good. He could hand fight, he could ride and he didn't panic in matches. He had a great demeanor and he was confident. I would get really nervous in big matches. I was proud I kept it that close. I was just hoping I didn't get embarrassed."

Dlagnev met the top-ranked Sigman again during the National Duals in Cleveland. Dlagnev executed a textbook duck under to score the opening takedown of the match. But Sigman, who was lethal in the top position, eventually wore Dlagnev down.

"I was up 2-1 after the first period and I chose down in the second period," Dlagnev said. "He rode me out. It was still 2-1 after the second period, but my arm was dead. In the third period, he kept hanging on my arm. He took it to me and I got my freaking butt kicked."

It was the second of nine meetings in college between Dlagnev and Sigman, who went on to become a four-time national champion.

"Sigman beat me nine times in college – I was 0-9 against him. And I am not sure I ever got away from him," Dlagnev said. "Sigman was two years older than me, and wrestling against him pushed me and motivated me.

"Back then, he was a lot bigger than me. I weighed around 215 or 220 my freshman year. He was around 255 or 260."

Dlagnev placed sixth at nationals as a freshman, but started closing the gap on Sigman the following season.

They met in the 2006 NCAA finals with Sigman seeking his fourth national title. Sigman won the match 1-0.

"I didn't want to go in the down position and I chose neutral," Dlagnev said. "He chose down and he was able to get an escape. That was the difference in the match. He played it super safe and he did what he needed to do to win that match. He was a great wrestler and a great opponent."

Dlagnev grew to 235 pounds for his junior season at UNK.

"I got bigger and stronger, and I was pretty dominant that season," he said. "And I was on track to win my first national title."

Dlagnev entered the 2007 national tournament, held that season at UNK, as a favorite to win an NCAA DII championship. But one wrestler Dlagnev had a tough time wrestling was Josh LeadingFox of Central Oklahoma.

"He gave me fits," Dlagnev said. "He had a flexing knee and he was hard to score on. We went into double overtime in the dual. I couldn't finish on him and it was exhausting. I finally took him down in overtime to win the match."

Dlagnev and LeadingFox advanced to the national championship match. But this time the bout wasn't as close.

"I snapped him to his face and got behind him in the first 10 seconds of the match," Dlagnev said. "I took him down again. He tried a Granby roll and I caught him on his back and pinned him."

Dlagnev jumped to his feet, raising his arms while jumping up and down as his home fans cheered.

"I was super excited," he said. "That was by far the most emotion I ever showed after a match. That was the first time I had whooped that guy. And that was the first time in my life that I had ever won my season-ending tournament. I had never won state and had never won nationals."

Dlagnev had won his first individual national title, but the Lopers had come up short of winning the team championship on their home mats.

"It was really disappointing as a team," he said. "We were ranked No. 1 going into nationals, but Central Oklahoma had a great tournament. They put five in the finals – three of those five guys got fourth in their regional."

Dlagnev also had excelled against NCAA Division I competition during the 2006-07 season. He had won the prestigious Midlands Championships. He defeated Northwestern's Dustin Fox, who went on to become an NCAA champion.

"I had some opportunities to transfer to a Division I school after my junior season," Dlagnev said. "I knew I wanted to wrestle after college. I also wanted to make sure I got my degree and I decided to finish it at UNK. I thought pretty seriously about transferring. But it was going to be hard to leave. If we would have won the team title in 2007, it would have been easier."

Bauer appreciated Dlagnev staying at Nebraska-Kearney.

"Tervel was being recruited left and right after he won nationals in 2007," Bauer said. "A bunch of Division I schools were recruiting him illegally. It shows you a lot about his character and his loyalty that he stayed. He had built great relationships with the guys on the UNK team."

A few weeks after winning an NCAA DII title, Dlagnev placed fourth in freestyle wrestling at the U.S. Open. That provided a boost for Dlagnev going into his senior year of college. Dlagnev returned for his final season at Nebraska-Kearney during the 2007-08 school year.

"We returned a bunch of guys," he said. "And we added Marty Usman. We had a good team, but we were much more inconsistent that year. I remember having to pin someone for us to win a dual."

Dlagnev's final NCAA Division II tournament turned into a closely contested battle between the Lopers and Minnesota State-Mankato.

"We won nationals by half a point," he said. "It came down to my finals match at heavyweight and all I had to do was win. I was pretty confident going into the finals. I wrestled a more controlled match. I took a lot of shots against Dustin Finn from UCO. I took him down toward the end and I won 4-1. I just didn't want to make any mistakes and do anything stupid."

Dlagnev won his second individual national title and

helped UNK win its first national team title in school history.

"It was awesome to win that championship," he said. "Winning with my friends, it was amazing. I remember talking with my teammates about being the first team to win it. It was like a dream come true. We actually did it. It was a great way to finish my college career."

Bauer appreciated the contributions Dlagnev made to the Loper program.

"Tervel was a great leader and a great teammate – he fit in so well with everyone in our program," Bauer said. "The guy was such a student of the sport – he watched every video he could get his hands on. He was so determined to succeed. He is a great technician and has one of the most intelligent wrestling minds we've ever seen.

"He always has been such a humble young man. He is truly an amazing individual who is so pleasant to be around. We were so fortunate and blessed to have him come through our program."

Dlagnev's entry into Senior level freestyle began in 2006. After falling to Sigman in the 2006 NCAA finals, Dlagnev met him again at the Northern Plains freestyle event.

They met in the first round. Dlagnev won by technical superiority in the first period before Sigman came back to win the next two periods to prevail in the best-of-3 period format.

"He won the match, but I actually outscored him 7-3 over the three periods," Dlagnev said. "I felt good about that."

Dlagnev decided to stay in Cedar Falls, Iowa after the Northern Plains event to train with World bronze medalist Tolly Thompson at the University of Northern Iowa. Thompson then invited Dlagnev to go with him to the U.S. Olympic Training Center in Colorado Springs, Colorado.

Dlagnev trained at the OTC for two weeks, wrestling against Olympian and future UFC champion Daniel Cormier. He also wrestled with NCAA champion Damion Hahn.

"I did well against those guys," Dlagnev said. "I took Damion down a couple times. I tech falled Cormier in the first period of a simulation match and nobody knew who I was. Kevin Jackson got up and yelled at everyone in the room after that. Then Cormier beat me 1-0, 2-0 in the last two periods. Having some success against those top wrestlers gave me a lot of confidence and made me super excited. That was the point when I knew that I really wanted to wrestle internationally."

Shortly after winning his second NCAA DII title, Dlagnev placed third at the U.S. Open against Senior level wrestlers in 2008.

Dlagnev had been training in Cedar Falls and joined the highly acclaimed Sunkist Kids Wrestling Club.

The day before he was scheduled to fly to Las Vegas for the Olympic Trials, Dlagnev drove four hours round trip to and from Des Moines. He went on a date with his future wife, Kirsten, at Texas Roadhouse in the Des Moines suburb of Urbandale. It was actually their first date. Kirsten was from Omaha and they had met while in school at UNK.

Dlagnev arrived back in Cedar Falls late that night before driving an hour to Cedar Rapids early the next morning to catch a flight to Las Vegas.

"I got very little sleep and then our flight got delayed," he said. "I was young and I was right out of college, and I wasn't managing my sleep or my diet very well at that point.

Dlagnev won his first match at the 2008 Olympic Trials, but he lost his next two and was eliminated from the tournament.

"My legs and arms were super heavy," he said. "I'm sure the lack of sleep didn't help me. It was disappointing, but I definitely learned a lesson from it."

Dlagnev rebounded to win the University Nationals. He went on to capture the 2008 University World title in Greece.

"At that point, I was really pumped," he said. "That was an important step in my career. Kevin Jackson, the U.S. National Coach, invited me to the Olympic Team training camps. That was important for me. I was able to train with the best guys in the country."

Dlagnev jumped right into freestyle wrestling full-time. And he made an immediate impact.

"I went to Russia on a tour in late 2008 and I went 0-1," he said. "I figured I was going to take my lumps."

Dlagnev's second trip was to Ukraine and Iran. He won the tournament in Ukraine and beat a past world medalist from Georgia. Dlagnev defeated a Ukranian world medalist and then lost to Iran's Fardin Massoumi, who had beaten American Steve Mocco in the Olympics.

"I got first and third on that tour. Then I medaled in an event in Bulgaria. Competing at that level wasn't as overwhelming as I thought. I started to have some success and build some confidence. Freestyle suited me better than folkstyle. My style adapted very quickly. I was at my best wrestling on my feet and that is mainly what you do in freestyle."

Dlagnev also needed to put on weight and muscle to compete against the best wrestlers on the planet.

"I eventually went from 235 pounds to about 265," he said. "And it was good weight. I was getting stronger. And I still had good mobility."

Dlagnev continued to wrestle well, advancing to the semifinals of the 2009 U.S. Open in Las Vegas. He earned a shot at facing a familiar foe, Sigman, in the semifinals.

Sigman won the first period before Dlagnev won the next two. Dlagnev scored a takedown to win the third period 1-0. He had defeated Sigman for the first time in his career.

"It was very dramatic," Dlagnev said. "That was a big win for me."

Dlagnev didn't have much time to celebrate. His finals opponent was Mocco, who had represented the U.S. at the 2008 Olympic Games.

"Mocco was always a little bit intimidating," Dlagnev said. "He was so strong and had great defense. He was hard to score on. At that point, I was still scared of him."

Dlagnev lost that match, but he earned another shot at Mocco during the finals of the 2009 World Team Trials in Council Bluffs, Iowa. They would meet in a best-of-3 match series with the winner advancing to the World Championships in Herning, Denmark. Dlagnev entered the final round series still a bit intimidated by Mocco.

"My mentality was 'this is great, I'm in the finals. But don't get embarrassed.' Then I won the first match, so now I am playing with house money," Dlagnev said. "I actually started to believe I could beat him."

Mocco rebounded to win the second match.

"I had a leg clinch and I couldn't finish," Dlagnev said. "I blew my opportunity to win the match and make the World Team. I went into the back and thought there was no chance."

But there was a chance. Dlagnev's coaches helped him regroup and he returned to the mat for the third and deciding match of the hard-fought series.

"I hit a high crotch and took Mocco to his back. I won the first period 3-1," Dlagnev said. "He got a pushout in the second period. Then I won a scramble and scored a point with four seconds left. I was like, 'Oh my God, I just made the World Team.'"

Dlagnev raised his arms in celebration. He had just made his first United States World Team.

"I blew my own mind," he said. "It was really exciting, but I also was very surprised. I wasn't totally convinced I could beat the guy. I probably gave Mocco a little too much respect. But that's kind of how my mind worked. I would have a lot of anxiety and doubt before matches."

Between the Trials and the Worlds, Dlagnev took another big step. He won the Golden Grand Prix in Azerbaijan.

Dlagnev tried to take full advantage of making his first World Team.

"Going through camps as the No. 1 guy, it was awesome," he said. "John Smith was the World Team coach. I had watched videos of him when I started wrestling. The legends of the sport were there to help me. It was a very surreal experience. I remember taking the team photo. I was very proud to wear USA and wear the red, white and blue colors. I was pumped and excited."

Dlagnev headed to the 2009 World Championships in Denmark and came out ready to go.

He defeated wrestlers from Hungary, Belarus and Azerbaijan to reach the semifinal round. He faced Massoumi, the Iranian wrestler he had lost to earlier in the season, and came up short in the World semis. But Dlagnev rebounded with a 2-0, 2-0 win over Georgia's Alex Modebadze.

Just a little more than a year after finishing his college career at UNK, Dlagnev had captured a World bronze medal.

"At that point, I became a World medalist and that was important for me," he said. "I knew I could compete with the best guys in the world."

Dlagnev followed by wrestling well at the World Cup. He was well on his way to reaching his goals.

Dlagnev had trained at Northern Iowa, but following

the 2009 World Championships he decided to move to Ohio State.

"They made a great offer," he said. "Plus, World Team members J.D. Bergman and Tommy Rowlands were there."

Dlagnev continued to excel internationally after the calendar flipped to 2010. But then something unexpected happened. He lost to Sigman in the finals of the U.S. Open.

"I was surprised because I thought I had passed him," Dlagnev said. "Then I lost to him again twice at the World Team Trials. He beat me in two straight matches. Losing to Sigman, it was a good learning experience. If you don't come with everything you have, these guys can beat you. I was very shocked. I learned a good lesson. I needed to compete really hard and fight. It recalibrated me."

Dlagnev had a busy 2010. He was married on May 10, 2010. He and his wife, Kirsten, had met during his last semester at UNK.

"We hit it off right away," he said. "She was a sophomore and I was a senior in college when we met. We went to the same church."

Dlagnev's wrestling was back on track in 2011. He made his second World Team. He also landed on a loaded half of the bracket at the World Championships in Istanbul, Turkey.

Dlagnev met Olympic and World champion Artur Taymazov of Uzbekistan in the quarterfinals of the 2011 Worlds. Dlagnev earned one of the biggest wins of his career in that bout. He prevailed in a gritty, hard-fought battle.

"I got beat up physically in that match," Dlagnev said. "I had neck pain for months."

Dlagnev dropped his next match before eventually finishing fifth. He fell short of medaling, but he qualified the weight class for the 2012 Olympic Games.

Now he needed to win the U.S. Olympic Trials to earn a trip to London. Dlagnev did exactly that, defeating Sigman in the finals to become an Olympian for the first time.

"That was the best I wrestled against him," he said. "I was very happy with it. It was awesome to become an Olympian."

Dlagnev had won the Olympic Trials, but there was one more hurdle to clear. He had to pass his drug test, which appeared to be a mere formality, to make the team.

"I was very nervous I was going to fail my USADA test," he said. "There were all these things running through my mind that I could maybe test positive for. That's just how I think sometimes. I didn't get the letter for five weeks and then I was finally notified I had passed the test. I was a guy that didn't smoke or drink, but I was still worried about it."

Dlagnev arrived in London and started training for the Olympics before being injured in practice.

"I was wrestling Jake Varner and he popped my rib," he said. "It was 17 days before competition, and I was in excruciating pain. I wasn't able to twist my core. I couldn't move for three or four days. Even nine days after I was injured, my rib was still bothering me. That really messed with me psychologically. I was super nervous. I kept dwelling on what was going to go wrong."

Dlagnev prepared to compete and still wasn't feeling 100 percent.

"The doctors shot me up in my ribs," he said, "so I could go out there and compete."

Dlagnev opened with a win over a wrestler from Egypt before knocking off returning world champion Aleksey Shemarov of Belarus in the quarterfinals. That set up a rematch with the powerful Taymazov in the semifinals.

Dlagnev went to his offense early in the match and shot in on a takedown attempt.

"I had a single leg on him," he said. "I was thinking they would call a stalemate and stop it. I maybe let up for a second, and he ran to the cradle and turned me over and pinned me."

It was a stunning end to a match that was expected to go the distance like it had the year before at the World Championships.

"I should've made him wrestle six minutes," Dlagnev said. "I lost by a pin in the first period at the Olympics. I knew how I let it happen. I was very frustrated with myself."

Dlagnev came back to face Iran's Komeil Ghasemi in the match for bronze.

"He had very flexible knees and he was hard to score on," Dlagnev said. "I finished fifth in the 2012 Olympics. It was disappointing. I had high expectations for that tournament."

Dlagnev came back strong the next year and was in

medal contention again in 2013. He lost in the bronze medal match and placed fifth at the World Championships.

"I was thinking 'I'm never going to medal again,'" he said.

That wasn't the case. Dlagnev rebounded to win a World bronze medal in 2014 in Tashkent, Uzbekistan. He lost a close match to Taha Akgul of Turkey in the quarterfinals. Akgul went on to win gold in that event.

"It was really cool to be back on the podium," he said. "I became a multiple World medalist for the United States."

The momentum from 2014 was short-lived. Dlagnev had back surgery in 2015.

"As a competitor, you always think you are going to be fine," he said. "But the back injury, that was really hard. I was in constant pain."

Dlagnev made his second U.S. Olympic Team in 2016, but he wasn't 100 percent physically. Not even close. But he was still trying to get himself ready to wrestle at the Olympic Games in Rio de Janeiro, Brazil.

"I wasn't able to do much wrestling or train hard for the three months before the Olympics," he said. "I couldn't train with anybody. I would tie my shoes and my core would spasm. I was depressed. The whole time over there was just a mess."

Dlagnev won his first two matches at the 2016 Olympics. He knocked off returning World silver medalist Jamaladdin Magomedov of Azerbaijan. He then earned a win over a wrestler from Poland in the quarterfinals.

"I won the match, but I hurt my back again," he said.

Dlagnev had just walked off the mat after his quarterfinal bout when his named was called again for a semifinal match against Ghasemi.

"I couldn't even get in a stance," Dlagnev said. "I didn't want to go back out there. Ghasemi snapped me and started to gut wrench me. He teched me. And then I went out for the bronze match and I got teched right away. I shouldn't have gone out there. I should've forfeited.

"I was 31 years old. I wasn't a kid. I knew I shouldn't have wrestled. I was in very, very bad pain."

It was a difficult conclusion to an excellent international career. Dlagnev made seven United States World and Olympic teams. But those years of battling some of the biggest and strongest wrestlers on the planet had taken their toll.

He stepped away from competition after 2016 as a two-time World bronze medalist. But that would later change.

Three years after retiring from wrestling, Dlagnev earned his highest achievement in the sport. In 2019, Dlagnev started receiving text messages from friends with a link that 2012 Olympic gold medalist Artur Taymazov of Uzbekistan had been disqualified from the event. Taymazov had been busted for a doping violation after retesting of samples from the 2012 Olympics.

"I started hearing rumors I was getting an Olympic medal," Dlagnev said. "(Taymazov) appealed it and then we had to wait for months for a final decision."

The news finally arrived. The International Olympic

Committee stripped Taymazov of his gold medal. That elevated Dlagnev from fifth to third place, making him an Olympic bronze medalist.

Davit Modzmanashvili of Georgia had been stripped of his Olympic silver medal in that same weight class earlier in the year.

"I got an email from Cody Bickley at USA Wrestling," Dlagnev said. "He informed me that I was going to get the medal. Ghasemi ended up winning gold and I got a bronze.

"It was cool and it was nice. USA Wrestling paid me for being the bronze medalist from their medal fund. I got a medalist bonus from USA Wrestling for $25,000. It was awesome and I was honored."

The timing of the violation was unexpected, but the result of the drug test wasn't.

"Taymazov was juicing the year before when I beat him at the Worlds in 2011," Dlagnev said. "I showed that there are ways to even beat the cheaters."

Dlagnev made eight U.S. National Teams from 2009-16 and was a two-time United States Olympian. He won an Olympic bronze medal and two World bronze medals for the American squad.

Dlagnev certainly has followed an interesting path that has taken him from Bulgaria to Austria, California, Texas, Nebraska, Ohio and then back to Nebraska.

"My road is unique," he said. "I was surrounded by a lot of great people who had an impact on me. I am proud of what I was able to accomplish. I am very grateful and blessed for what wrestling allowed me to do with my life."

Dlagnev has continued to make a major impact in the sport. He served as an assistant coach at Ohio State University before being hired as an assistant at the University of Nebraska. Dlagnev and his wife are raising their three children in Lincoln.

"I love Nebraska," he said. "It's a great place and I really enjoy it. I have a lot of great memories from being in this state. It is a place that feels like home for me."

It has been more than two decades now since Dlagnev came to the state of Nebraska for the first time.

"I love the University of Nebraska-Kearney," he said. "I love the place – it was a great school and a great community for me. I still go back and reminisce. Coach Bauer was a blessing for me. My best friends to this day are guys that I met at UNK. Having that be a piece of my story is a great honor.

"I always keep up with the wrestling program and follow them to see how they are doing. I will text Coach Jensen at nationals to keep tabs on them."

Dlagnev's time at Nebraska-Kearney certainly was memorable.

"It was an amazing experience at UNK," he said. "I did a lot of growing up during my time there. I matured so much. There were great people there who were extremely positive. I will never forget the time I spent there. It is a special place, that's for sure."

CHAPTER 6
BREAKING THROUGH

You often hear wrestling coaches talking about it – every point matters in a big wrestling tournament. Scoring bonus and advancement points are critical when teams are locked in a close race while trying to win an important championship. Never was that more evident than at the 2008 NCAA Division II Championships in Cedar Rapids, Iowa.

The team race was expected to be close with Nebraska-Kearney, Minnesota State-Mankato, Nebraska-Omaha and Central Oklahoma among the top teams expected to battle for the title.

"We were ranked fourth nationally going into the tournament," UNK coach Marc Bauer said. "I am not sure we were even considered a contender for the team title. We knew Brett Allgood and Tervel Dlagnev had a chance to win titles. Mankato was the favorite going into it."

The Lopers turned out to be more than contenders. They entered the finals leading by half a point over Minnesota State. UNK had two wrestlers competing in the finals and the Mavericks had three.

Minnesota State was up first at 125 pounds, but Nick Smith dropped an 8-2 decision to UNO's Cody Garcia in the title bout. Allgood was up next for UNK. He came through at 133 pounds, earning a hard-fought 5-3 finals win over Shane Perkey of Indianapolis.

Allgood's win boosted the Lopers to a 104.5 to 100 lead over Minnesota State. The Mavericks came right back with victories from Jason Rhoten at 157 pounds and Andy Pickar at 165 pounds to take a 108 to 104.5 lead in the team race.

The tournament and the team race came down to the final bout at heavyweight. Dlagnev, the returning national champion, took the mat to face Central Oklahoma's Dustin Finn. A victory by Dlagnev would be worth four points and give the Lopers the championship.

Dlagnev came through with a 4-1 victory to give Nebraska-Kearney its first national team title in school history. The Lopers edged Minnesota State 108.5 to 108 for the championship. Every point, and every half point in this case, definitely mattered at the 2008 DII nationals.

"When Tervel came off the stage, the first thing he did was embrace the team and the team embraced him," Bauer said. "It was a pretty cool moment. It was really special."

The finals matches were critical, but Nebraska-Kearney also came through on the back side of the bracket. UNK's Ryan Etherton recovered from a loss in the quarterfinals, winning four straight matches to place third at 149. He recorded a major decision and two falls before winning by decision in the third-place bout. Those bonus points obviously were needed.

Joe Ellenberger also delivered for the Lopers at 157 pounds, navigating a difficult journey after suffering a first-round setback to UNO's Henry Wahle. Ellenberger came back to win five straight matches to place third. He won one bout by major decision and two others in overtime.

UNK's Kamaru Usman also scored important team points at 174 pounds. Usman came back from a loss in the semifinals to win his next two matches to place third. He won by a major decision in his first match of the tournament.

Jeff Rutledge also placed third for the Lopers at 141 pounds. He came back from a semifinal setback to win his final two matches of the tournament.

UNK also had All-Americans in Keenan McCurdy (165) and Derek Ross (197). Both wrestlers won two matches apiece while placing eighth in the tournament.

Nebraska-Kearney's Paul Sutton won only one match at 184 pounds, but it was an important victory. He won by a major decision.

"Winning the school's first national championship was hard for us to believe because we weren't favored to win," Bauer said. "We had nine qualifiers, so we knew if we had a strong tournament there was a chance.

"It wasn't until the consolation quarterfinals that we knew we had a chance. We punched four wrestlers into the consolation finals, pulling out two huge upsets that secured a team trophy with eight All-Americans and two national finalists."

Nebraska-Kearney came together, scratching and clawing to score every necessary point in becoming the first Loper wrestling team to capture a national championship.

"That team was very special – all nine wrestlers contributed at nationals," Bauer said. "Our 184-pounder was the only wrestler who wasn't an All-American, but he won a match. Everyone contributed to that national championship.

"I loved that team. They were dedicated and committed to putting the work in. Each of them brought something different to the team but they always found a way to pull together and support each other."

The Lopers finally broke through and won a national team title.

"It was huge for our program," Bauer said. "We felt like in 2006 we had honed a process of peaking our guys at the right time. We wanted to make guys the most efficient at the end of the year. It really started showing.

"We were ranked No. 1 the entire season in 2007. We were the favorite and ended up finishing second at home to Central Oklahoma. It was disappointing. It definitely was motivation for those guys in 2008. It was tough not winning it in 2007. We had some tough matches early. Finishing second, it lit a fire under us. That pushed us to win it the next year.

"Winning the championship in 2008, we felt like we had a great process for training our student athletes. We went second, second and first at nationals. We figured out how to get them to peak. Every point matters. That was proven in that tournament. Once you win a championship, people want to be a part of that success. It really helped with recruiting. We could sell our program."

CHAPTER 7
THE NIGERIAN NIGHTMARE

Kamarudeen Usman's path to a college wrestling room in Kearney, Nebraska was hardly conventional. And highly unlikely. He overcame numerous obstacles and his share of adversity to achieve his goals.

Usman was born in Nigeria and spent the first eight years of his life in the African country. Then his father, Muhammed, made the decision to move his family to the United States. The Usmans settled in Dallas, Texas. Kamaru later attended Bowie High School in the Dallas suburb of Arlington.

Usman made what turned out to be a life-altering decision when he was a sophomore in high school. He joined the wrestling team. Usman was a fast learner. He picked the sport up quickly and started to have success.

Usman finished with a 53-3 record as a prep senior and placed third in the Texas state high school tournament. He drew the attention of Appalachian State, an NCAA Division I school.

At that time, Usman also had been hearing about a

heavyweight wrestler from Arlington named Tervel Dlagnev, who was excelling at the NCAA Division II level for the University of Nebraska at Kearney.

"Tervel was hitting his stride and doing really well," Usman said. "I recognized that he was doing well at a school up in Nebraska. At the time, I didn't really know much about Kearney or even where it was.

"It was all about Division I for me. I wanted to wrestle at that level. My hopes were all about going DI. I was starting to have some good results and I was gaining confidence. I was falling in love with the sport of wrestling."

Usman said he was a decent student in high school with a grade-point average just under 3.0. But his test scores fell short of gaining admission to an NCAA Division I school.

Instead of going DI, Usman elected to pursue another path. He wound up at William Penn University, an NAIA school in Oskaloosa, Iowa.

"I redshirted my first year in college, but I quickly realized in practice that I could compete with these guys," Usman said. "We were still allowed to compete in open tournaments and I was doing pretty well."

Following that first year at William Penn, Usman decided he needed to make a move.

"I eventually decided that I wanted to transfer to Nebraska-Kearney, but the William Penn coaches wouldn't release me to go there," Usman said. "That obviously was frustrating and disappointing, but there wasn't anything I could do at that point."

Usman returned to William Penn the following season and tried to make the best of his situation.

"I started doing really well my second year of college," he said. "I got to the semifinals of the Cyclone Open. I beat a couple of college All-Americans. I beat Ross Taplin, who was a two-time All-American at Nebraska-Omaha. I beat a recruit from Iowa.

"I wrestled Travis Paulson (an All-American from Iowa State) and lost 3-1 in overtime in the semis. That was kind of my coming out party that year. It let me know I could compete at this level."

Usman went on to excel in the postseason in 2007. He won the conference tournament and beat his William Penn teammate, who was a two-time NAIA All-American. NAIA schools were allowed to enter more than one wrestler in a weight class in the national qualifying meet.

Usman was hitting his peak and ready to take aim at winning a national championship. But then disaster struck, most notably some bad weather as the team embarked on its trip to Sioux Falls, South Dakota for nationals.

"A huge storm hit on our way up there – it was snowing really hard, the wind was blowing and you couldn't even see the road," Usman said. "We were two hours away from Sioux Falls and we had to stop and get a hotel."

The William Penn team was scrambling to find its way to the tournament. One of the coaches had a truck he thought could make it to Sioux Falls, but said he only had room for four wrestlers in it. Usman was one of the wrestlers left behind.

"I missed the national tournament," he said. "The coach decided to take the guy in my weight class who I had just beaten. He ended up placing third at nationals. I think I could've won the national title, but we will never know. I think they took the other kid because he was a senior."

Usman was more convinced than ever that it was time to make a change. He couldn't leave William Penn soon enough after everything that transpired. He packed his bags and headed west. He was about to enter three of the most pivotal and important years of his life. Usman enrolled at the University of Nebraska at Kearney.

"It was one of the best decisions I ever made," he said. "I was building the skill and building the technique as a wrestler during the two years at William Penn. And I took my wrestling to a whole new level when I got to UNK."

When Usman arrived in central Nebraska, he made a quick observation.

"I was one of only two Black kids on the team," he said. "I felt a little out of place when I first went to Kearney."

But that quickly changed.

"Tervel really helped me fit in – we both had that Texas and Arlington connection," Usman said. "The coaches were great, and all of the guys on the team were super friendly and welcoming. It was a really good group of guys and they really embraced me when I got there.

"The wrestlers at Nebraska-Kearney loved wrestling and they wanted to be successful. It was like a small family of hard working and God-fearing individuals. Coach Bauer was on board with me coming in there."

Usman received another chance to learn about his new teammates during a trip in the summer of 2007.

"UNK had a team trip set up to Germany and Iceland," Usman said. "I went with the team, and it was an amazing trip. We did a lot of wrestling and I bonded with the team. It was the first time I had traveled out of the United States as a young adult.

"We were there for two weeks. We wrestled in a tournament. It was a fantastic trip and we had a chance to experience some different cultures. It didn't take long to realize that my teammates were just a great group of guys. Everyone wanted to improve and get better. And they all wanted to win. It lit a fire under me. I was around guys who had the same goals I had."

Usman was looking at earning the starting spot for UNK at 174 pounds for the 2007-08 season. But he had trouble making the starting lineup.

"We had our Blue and Gold wrestle-off before the season, and I got beat by the starter from the previous year," Usman said. "Paul Sutton beat me 7-5 in the wrestle-off. I remember feeling so crappy after losing. I couldn't believe that I got beat in the wrestle-off. I was supposed to be helping them win the national title, but then I lost to my teammate."

Usman followed by wrestling at the Cowboy Open in Wyoming. He went 2-2 and felt like he wasn't wrestling to his full potential.

"I called my high school coach and I was crying and upset," Usman said. "I told him that I didn't have it anymore and I was going to quit wrestling. I was upset and pissed off. I told him I was working just as hard in practice as everyone else, but not getting the results I wanted.

"My high school coach then responded with a message that really resonated with me. He said, 'If you're doing the same thing as everyone else in practice, why do you expect to do better than them?'

"I had a mindset switch at that point to do something extra to get to the goals I wanted to achieve. I started doing extra work and it eventually paid off for me."

Usman's mind was right, but he still wasn't the starter.

"The team was flying to Las Vegas for the Cliff Keen Invitational, which was a huge tournament with a lot of top Division I wrestlers in it," Usman said. "But I didn't go. They took Paul Sutton to Vegas because he had beaten me when we wrestled.

"I ended up missing out on a great trip and a great tournament. I wasted a great opportunity to compete in Vegas."

Instead of going to Las Vegas to compete, Usman flew back to Texas.

"I went home for Thanksgiving. I was really licking my wounds," he said. "I was home with my parents, eating turkey over Thanksgiving. But during the break, I tried to make the most of my time. I worked out really hard. I was determined to come back strong after a disappointing start to the season."

The following week, Usman was back on the mat for a tournament in Fort Hays, Kansas. And ready to make a big splash.

"That was a turning point in my athletic career," Usman said. "I ended up winning the tournament and beating two All-Americans that were ranked. That set the tone for the rest of the season and the rest of my career in college."

The following week, Usman capped the pre-Christmas schedule by competing in the tournament on his home mats at Nebraska-Kearney.

"I made it to the finals and I was able to beat Sutton 7-4 to win it," Usman said. "I didn't look back after that."

The Lopers followed by competing in the prestigious Midlands Championships, another big tournament with numerous top Division I wrestlers. It was one of the toughest college tournaments in the country and was held at Northwestern. Usman had high hopes for that event, but they were quickly dashed.

"I tore the meniscus in my knee. My season was potentially over," he said. "I talked to a surgeon and I told him I wanted to keep wrestling. I had surgery – they did a scope on my knee. I wasn't able to return again until our conference tournament."

Usman wasn't 100 percent physically, but he tried to make the best of a difficult situation. The Lopers had designs on winning a national team title and Usman's contributions were going to be needed.

"I came back and won our conference to qualify for nationals," Usman said. "I was ranked No. 1 going into the national tournament in Cedar Rapids, Iowa."

Usman won his first two matches at the 2008 NCAA Division II Championships before running into Albert Miles of Pitt-Johnstown in the semifinals. Miles prevailed 6-2.

"I had never seen the kid before plus I was just coming off surgery on my knee," Usman said. "I had a huge brace on my right knee and I was pretty limited, especially on my feet. I couldn't push off or get in my stance. It was tough to shoot and get to my offense because of my knee. I had to change my style and do what I could to win."

Usman had little time to feel sorry for himself after the loss.

"I was completely demoralized after the semifinals. I wasn't happy and I was down, but then I had to come right back and wrestle on the back side of the bracket," he said. "I was pissed off because I couldn't wrestle the way I wanted to with my knee not being 100 percent.

"I managed to come back and win my next two matches and place third. I really had to dig deep to do that. I knew I needed to come back and become an All-American to help our team."

Usman's wins were critical as the Lopers ended up edging Minnesota State-Mankato by half a point to win the first national team title in wrestling in UNK history.

"Our whole team really came through," Usman said. "It was a great feeling to win the team title. We had a close-knit team and everybody really stepped up and delivered. Obviously, every match and every point mattered.

"Tervel had a close match in the finals. He came through with a win to give us the championship. He set himself apart. He was beating everybody. He won Midlands that year. He was undefeated that season. He was becoming a force and beating a lot of top DI guys."

Usman came back even more determined for his junior season during the 2008-09 school year. Among his toughest opponents was Brett Hunter, a national champion who also wrestled for a Nebraska college. Hunter competed for Chadron State.

Usman had the upper hand against Hunter during the season and was in control late in the 2009 conference finals.

"There were 20 seconds left in the match, and I was on top and was riding him out," Usman said. "He reached down and grabbed two of my fingers and I tore my index finger tendon on my left hand. It ruptured completely. I didn't realize how bad it was at first because I had so much adrenaline. But I knew something was wrong. I won the match. I majored him, but I ended up with a pretty serious injury."

Two weeks later, Usman headed to the 2009 national tournament in Houston with a large wrap around his left hand.

"It was tough – it really limited me," he said. "I had no grip with that hand and I couldn't do much of anything. Guys were grabbing my hand and squeezing it because it was taped up. It was difficult and it was painful, but I tried to make the best of it."

Usman won three matches to land a spot in the finals against a familiar foe. He would face Hunter again, this time with a national title at stake at 174 pounds.

"I ended up losing to Hunter 3-2 in the finals on riding time," Usman said. "That was really frustrating. It was a very tough pill to swallow."

Usman had one last opportunity to become a national champion during his senior season at UNK. That chance came at the 2010 NCAA meet in Omaha.

"I had vengeance on my mind – I wasn't going to lose to anybody," Usman said. "I wanted to kick the crap out of everybody I wrestled. I went 44-1 that season. My one loss was to Stephen Dwyer from Nebraska. He was a Division I All-American. I had beaten Ben Bennett from Central Michigan, who was a DI All-American."

Usman powered into the finals for the second straight year before earning a hard-fought 5-4 win over Luke Rynish of Wisconsin Parkside in the NCAA finals. He had captured a national championship.

Overcome with emotion, Usman dropped to his knees and celebrated after the final seconds ticked off the clock.

"It was what I had been working for the past three years. It was long overdue," he said. "It was exciting to finally do it and reach my goal. It was definitely a big relief and a great way to end my college career.

"I became the first Black wrestler to win a national title at the school. There have been a bunch of guys who have followed me after that, including Romero Cotton (who would win three national titles for the Lopers)."

Just a few hours after standing atop the medal podium, Usman had a chance to relax and reflect on what had just happened.

"After I won the national title in Omaha, I was in the hotel bar after the tournament and our team was celebrating," he said. "We didn't win as a team and I didn't like that. I had two sips of a rum and a coke. I started thinking, 'What's next?' And then I thought, 'Let's go win the Olympics.' That's what started the freestyle journey for me. I jumped right in and started training for freestyle wrestling."

Usman cut down to 163 pounds and entered the U.S. Open a month later. He won his first three matches before running into Travis Paulson, a wrestler who later made a U.S. World Team.

"I took Paulson to three periods and held my own fairly well," Usman said. "I remember Brandon Slay, one of the Team USA coaches, came up and talked to me after the tournament. I knew Brandon was from Texas and he was an Olympic champion. Brandon asked me to come to the Olympic Training Center to train in 2010."

Usman would spend the next two years training in freestyle wrestling at the United States Olympic Training Center in Colorado Springs.

"I had a lot of ups and downs," he said. "I was a Division II athlete and it was tough to gain that respect because most of the wrestlers out there had competed at DI schools. I think I had the talent. I was beating some good wrestlers in the room. I was having good matches with Keith Gavin and Andy Hrovat and putting pressure on them. Those guys were Division I All-Americans."

Usman received an opportunity to represent the United States at the 2010 University World Championships in Torino, Italy. He won his first match before finishing eighth. But Usman was unable to break through against top Senior level competition.

"I struggled in freestyle and starting having some injuries," he said. "I felt like I was always falling behind. I missed training and that set me back. I didn't feel like I could ever catch up. It ultimately broke my wrestling spirit."

A turning point for Usman came in 2011.

"I had a weekend off from wrestling," he said. "I got invited to go up to Denver and roll with some mixed martial arts guys. I went to a gym to train with some fighters. Muhammad Lawal, who they called King Mo, was there. Mo was the Strike Force champion. Rashad Evans was the UFC champion and he walked in. I worked out with Rashad. He told me, 'Wrestlers can thrive in this sport and you can do this.'

"I was actually beating Rashad in a wrestling workout. He hadn't been a wrestler for a few years, but for me, that built my confidence. We exchanged information and we talked after that."

Usman continued to wrestle through the end of the 2012 Olympic cycle, but his heart was no longer in it.

"I fell short of my goals in freestyle," he said. "But I was already checked out and had already started to fall in love with MMA."

Usman adapted well to mixed martial arts, which combines several disciplines that include wrestling, grappling, boxing, and kickboxing.

"It didn't take me long to transition into MMA – I went 110 percent into fighting," he said. "After falling short in freestyle, I was determined to excel in this new sport. I had success early. I was a high level wrestler coming into a sport that didn't have a lot of wrestlers. That gave me an advantage.

"I was so well-conditioned from wrestling and that gave me a big edge in MMA. Wrestling is the main component for fighting."

Usman entered the world of MMA with high expectations.

"Right off the bat, I set a goal of being a champion," he said. "I didn't know how I was going to do it, but I set a goal of winning a world title. That was the goal – 100 percent. I wanted to be a champion.

"I just kept building momentum. I started winning and my confidence kept growing. I had to pick up the sport fast. Fighting, you can really get beat up. You had to learn really fast or you wouldn't last long."

Usman made a steady progression in MMA and ultimately earned a shot at reaching his goal.

On March 2, 2019, Usman had a 15-1 record when he stepped into the Octagon in Las Vegas, Nevada. He was about to square off against Tyron Woodley, another former wrestler, for the Ultimate Fighting Championships welterweight title.

Usman controlled the five-round fight and dominated Woodley en route to prevailing by unanimous decision. Kamaru Usman had captured a UFC world title.

"The feeling when I won was amazing," he said. "I followed the same exact formula I did in college. I put so much hard work into it to win a championship. I was on my knees celebrating after I won the UFC title – I did the same thing when I won a national title at Kearney. I visualized that moment. When it actually happens, it is an incredible feeling. It is so fulfilling and rewarding to work so hard for a goal and finally achieve it."

Usman said there was no magic formula. He simply put the time and effort in to be successful.

"I attribute it to my work ethic," he said. "I just trusted it and I did it. I really learned that when I was at UNK. Coach Bauer had this quote posted in his office that said, "If you fail to plan, you plan to fail." Once I understood that, I wanted to have a plan for success. I did whatever it took to have success."

Usman held the UFC title belt for more than three years. He successfully defended his championship five times.

On August 20, 2022 in Salt Lake City, Usman met Leon Edwards in a rematch of their 2015 fight. Usman won the first fight and looked to be on course to win again. But Usman lost the fight via knockout late in the fifth round. It was his first loss in the UFC.

Usman, who turned 37 in 2024, also has served as a UFC analyst on ESPN and appeared in the Black Panther movie sequel.

He is now recognized worldwide from his success in the UFC and he has more than one million followers on X (formerly known as Twitter).

Even with all the years he has spent as a fighter, Usman replies quickly when asked what sport is the most challenging.

"Wrestling is harder than MMA, without a doubt," he said. "You have to be able to control an opponent to win a match. There are so many components to that. You have to have so many skills and techniques that go into being successful in wrestling."

UNK coach Marc Bauer said Usman – known as Marty during his Loper days – "fit in pretty well from the jump" after he arrived in Kearney.

"He worked extremely hard," Bauer said. "He obviously was very talented. But he pushed himself and never backed down from anybody. That's what made him special. Marty is an intelligent guy. He's very smart. He's very focused and driven."

Bauer said he was not surprised Usman went on to win a UFC title.

"Marty figured it out pretty quickly," Bauer said. "Having good wrestling technique helped him. He became a really good boxer and striker. When he won the UFC title, we were all excited. We were all texting each other. It was amazing. It was really cool. Everybody was proud of him. It was incredible to see him become a world champion."

Usman also has given back to the UNK program.

"Marty helped out with the fundraiser for the new

wrestling room," Bauer said. "He donated significantly for that. We really appreciated him doing that."

Usman said becoming a UFC champion likely would not have happened if he hadn't transferred to the University of Nebraska at Kearney in 2007.

"UNK flipped that switch to get me to that next level," Usman said. "I developed the work ethic and mindset that led me to success down the road. It paved the way for me."

Usman said he looks back fondly on the three years he spent as a student-athlete at Nebraska-Kearney.

"I still have that bond with those guys that I wrestled with at UNK," he said. "It's a school and a wrestling program that is always in my heart. I have a lot of love and loyalty for Nebraska-Kearney.

"When they needed help with their fundraiser, I was available. It is a family that I am always connected to and will be for the rest of my life."

Usman said he developed a close relationship with UNK teammate Joe Ellenberger, who also fought in the UFC.

"We still keep in contact," Usman said. "Joe introduced me to MMA. The first time I went to a live event was watching Joe compete in Omaha. Joe was very talented. If it wasn't for his injury, and he could've stayed healthy, he would've done really well in the UFC. He was the ultimate competitor. Joe was the glue on our team at UNK. He was a great teammate. He was tough as nails."

Usman still keeps tabs on the Loper wrestling program.

"It is always great to see how well the team at Nebraska-Kearney is still doing," he said. "Coach Bauer set the tone and built a powerhouse program. He knew how to run a successful program. He brought in good kids and built a great culture. It really was a family. He put the pieces together to have success.

"They have continued to have success with Dalton Jensen as the head coach. I have very fond memories from my time there. My time at Kearney provided the foundation that led me to be successful in my career."

LOPER LEGACY

Brian Hagan celebrates after becoming the first national champion in Loper wrestling history in 1990.

Alireza Amiri-Eliasi, who grew up in Iran, was a two-time national champion for the Lopers in 1990 and 1991.

Frank Kuchera overcame his share of adversity to become a two-time All-American for UNK in 2002 and 2003.

Senior Frank Kuchera celebrates after capturing an NCAA Division II title in 2003 in Wheeling, West Virginia.

LOPER LEGACY

Nebraska native Jeff Sylvester won a national title for the Lopers.

Tervel Dlagnev won national titles in 2007 and 2008, leading the Lopers to their first NCAA championship in 2008. He went on to win an Olympic bronze medal for the United States.

UNK coach
Marc Bauer with
heavyweight
Tervel Dlagnev

Tervel Dlagnev celebrates with coaches Marc Bauer
and Ty Swarm.

Dlagnev battles Artur Taymazov at the 2012 Olympic Games in London.

Dlagnev walks into the arena for a match at the 2012 Olympics.

Dlagnev with American coaches at the 2016 Olympic
Games in Rio de Janeiro, Brazil.

Dlagnev battles an opponent at the 2016 Olympics.

Brett Allgood
celebrates with
coaches Ty Swarm
and Marc Bauer.

Brett Allgood captured two national championships at 133 pounds for Nebraska-Kearney.

Kamarudeen Usman won a national title for the Lopers in 2010. He went on to become a world champion in the Ultimate Fighting Championships.

Kamaru Usman celebrates a UFC victory in 2021.

Usman in the cage
during a UFC title
bout.

Usman connects on a punch against Colby Covington
in 2021.

Usman steps into the ring before a UFC matchup.

Usman taunts an opponent in the ring during a 2021 fight.

(above) Raufeon Stots won a pair of national titles for the Lopers.

Stots hugs coaches Marc Bauer and Dalton Jensen in the corner.

LOPER LEGACY

Coaches Bauer and Jensen celebrate a Loper victory.

T.J. Hepburn
celebrates a
national title with
Coach Marc Bauer
cheering in the
background.

Dalton Jensen capped his college career with a national title for the Lopers in 2012.

Romero Cotton was a four-time NCAA finalist and three-time champion for UNK.

LOPER LEGACY

Daniel DeShazer was a four-time All-American, winning two national titles for the Lopers.

Daniel DeShazer celebrates after capturing a national title.

Destin McCauley won a national title for Nebraska-Kearney.

Keith Surber captured a national title for UNK.

Matt Malcom won a pair of national championships
for the Lopers.

Austin Eldredge wins a national championship
for UNK in 2023.

UNK coaches
(from left)
Tom McCann,
Andrew
Sorenson and
Dalton
Jensen.

Coaches Dalton Jensen and Zach Ondrak.

CHAPTER 8
THE NAME IS DALTON

Dalton Jensen grew up in southwest Iowa. He was raised in the small town of Missouri Valley, located just east of Omaha, Nebraska.

His father, Tom, excelled as a high school wrestler at Lincoln Southeast. He finished third at the Nebraska state tournament as a senior. Tom Jensen went on to wrestle collegiately for Kearney State. He qualified for the national tournament and landed a spot in the NAIA Championships at 142 pounds.

Dalton has two older brothers who were successful wrestlers for Missouri Valley High School. Jeremy Jensen is eight years older than Dalton and Keefer is five years older.

"My brothers had quite a bit of an impact on me," Dalton said. "They were a few years older. I was very impressionable. I thought my brothers were superstars, and I really looked up to them."

Jeremy Jensen won his share of matches while falling just short of qualifying for state. Keefer placed fifth at state as a junior and senior in Iowa. He was a national qualifier for Southwest Minnesota State in NCAA Division II. Keefer is now the head coach at Missouri Valley High School.

"They have been doing well," Dalton said of his alma mater. "They have qualified for state duals a handful of times."

Dalton Jensen's entry into wrestling came at a young age. He started when he was 4 years old. By seventh grade, he was fully immersed into the sport. Jensen said he was "pretty small" coming up through the ranks. He was wrestling opponents who were the same size, but that didn't always go well.

"I didn't handle losing early from a young age," he said. "I would throw tantrums. I was being too competitive. I would pull my headgear down and cry."

Jensen stuck with wrestling and started to enjoy more success. He placed in the top four in the AAU state tournament from third through eighth grade.

"I never won it. I got second once. I had a handful of third and fourth place finishes," he said. "It was frustrating. I loved wrestling and I wanted to win. I put in a lot of time for someone that age. I cared a lot."

Jensen entered high school weighing well below the lowest weight class of 103 pounds. He weighed just 90 pounds. Jensen was undersized, but he still managed to qualify for state as a freshman before coming up short of placing.

Jensen carried the momentum into the summer, becoming an All-American at USA Wrestling's Cadet Nationals. His progression continued as a high school sophomore.

Now a full-sized 103-pounder, Jensen powered into the 2005 state tournament with a No. 1 state ranking. He advanced to the finals before earning a 15-0 technical fall over Ridge Kiley of Eagle Grove. Jensen had captured a state championship.

"It was great to win state and I had worked hard for it. It was an expectation that I had. It wasn't a surprise, but it was a culmination of a lot of time put in," Jensen said. "The Iowa state tournament is something special. It was the last year for it being held at Vets Auditorium in Des Moines."

Jensen also made history for his school. He became Missouri Valley's first state champion in wrestling.

"It was gratifying," he said. "I remember growing up and watching state and watching my brother compete there. I had envisioned myself wrestling there. Vets Auditorium was a special place. It was really neat to win it there. It was something special, that's for sure."

Jensen bumped up to 119 pounds for his junior season. He was ranked No. 1 in the state all season. He won a pair of matches to reach the semifinal round at the state tournament. Jensen came out strong, building a 4-0 lead over Jace Thompson of Mason City Newman in the semis. But Thompson came back and rallied for a 6-5 upset victory.

"I had beat the second ranked kid in the quarters and I got off to a good start in the semis," Jensen said. "Thompson ended up winning it. Looking back on that loss in the semis, I kind of mentally collapsed in that match. I am not sure if I took it for granted. I jumped from 103 to 119 that season, and the physical maturity worked against me a little bit. At the time, I felt like it was the worst thing that was ever going to happen to me.

"I was pretty stunned, but I had to get ready to wrestle back after that loss. I came back to place third. I got a tech fall and a pin in my last two matches. I was a shell of myself after that match. It was hard to regroup. It takes character to come back after a tough loss like that. I was going to walk out and get the job done. The goal was gone at that point."

That loss served as motivation for Jensen.

"I used that loss to fuel me," he said. "I hung the third-place state medal from the rafters in my bedroom. It was a reminder of what happened."

Jensen suffered another setback over the summer when he failed to place at USA Wrestling's Junior Nationals in Fargo, North Dakota. That was a pivotal event with a number of college coaches there to look at prospects.

"Not placing, that didn't help with recruiting," he said.

Jensen decided to bump up one weight class to 125 pounds for his senior season at Missouri Valley. He suffered an early season loss, dropping a bout when he moved up to 130 for the Boys Town Tournament.

Jensen didn't lose again. He rolled into his final state tournament in 2007 determined to not let history repeat itself. He pinned three opponents in the first period en route to capturing his second state championship. He was named outstanding wrestler of the tournament. Jensen capped his career by pinning West Branch's Brad Exline in just 75 seconds.

"I came back a lot stronger after losing that match my junior year," he said. "That really motivated me my senior year."

Jensen continued to excel that summer. He won Junior Nationals in Greco-Roman wrestling before placing fourth in freestyle. His performance caught the attention of numerous college coaches, including Iowa State, Nebraska, Nebraska-Omaha and Nebraska-Kearney.

Iowa State coach Cael Sanderson, a four-time undefeated NCAA champion and Olympic gold medalist, offered Jensen a scholarship.

"That was a pretty easy decision to go to Iowa State, especially with Cael there," Jensen said. "I was a Husker fan and my heart wanted me to go to Lincoln. UNO and UNK would've been good fits for me. But when Cael Sanderson calls and comes and sits at your home, that was really appealing for me. Iowa State had just finished second at nationals. Cael was my idol. I wrote book reports on him. You don't say no to that guy. I committed on the spot. I had done a recruiting visit a few weeks before.

"Cael said, 'We're so excited to have you.' Everything felt right. How lucky was I to be going to wrestle for a guy like him? It was like a dream come true and like a fairy tale. After I won state my senior year, I went on a visit in March. He came to my house in the spring of 2007 and that's when I committed to Iowa State."

Jensen redshirted his first year at Iowa State.

"I was getting my butt kicked in the room," he said. "Nick Fanthorpe, Nick Gallick and Mitch Mueller were taking it to me. I had some really good training partners. Two of those guys were All-Americans. I put in a lot of time and I was working hard. But those guys were really good. I was just trying to scratch and claw my way to getting a takedown against them. I didn't realize the gap was going to be that big when I went to college."

Jensen did have success outside the Cyclone wrestling room. He built his confidence by winning two open tournaments during his redshirt season.

"I filled in a couple times on varsity my redshirt freshman year," Jensen said. "We had a really good lineup at Iowa State and it was tough to get in there."

Jensen placed sixth at the prestigious Midlands Championships that season. He lost to Wisconsin's Zach Tannelli, who placed fourth at NCAAs. He also lost to teammate Nick Gallick in the consolation semis. Gallick took third at NCAAs. Jensen also lost to Old Dominion's Ryan Williams, who finished second at nationals.

Shortly after the season, Jensen and his Cyclone teammates received stunning and shocking news. Cael Sanderson was leaving the head coaching position at Iowa State to take over the program at Penn State.

"That was a huge surprise," Jensen said. "It came out of nowhere. We never would have thought in a million years that Cael would have left Iowa State. I always had a good relationship with him and I still do. He took advantage of a great opportunity and knew what it was going to take to create a dynasty. I was a little bit bitter at first. There was some confusion and I didn't understand why it was happening."

Kevin Jackson, a past Cyclone All-American and Olympic gold medalist, was hired to replace Sanderson as head coach at Iowa State. Jackson had previously served as the U.S. National Freestyle Coach.

Jensen landed a starting spot as a Cyclone sophomore, taking over as the team's top 141-pounder. He qualified for the 2010 NCAA Division I Championships, where he went 1-2. Jensen had a .500 record during an up-and-down season.

"I think I went 27 days in January and February without winning during our dual meet season," he said. "I wrestled Kyle Dake of Cornell that year. He was a true freshman. He beat me 6-1. He rode me a lot."

Dake went on to win four NCAA titles and became a multi-time World champion in freestyle wrestling for the United States.

Jensen did earn a win over third-ranked Alex Krum of Maryland at the National Duals and defeated top-10 ranked Ryan Prater of Illinois. Jensen also wrestled tough against top-ranked Reece Humphrey of Ohio State before dropping a 6-5 decision. Humphrey later placed fifth at the World Championships.

Jensen definitely was competitive that season at the NCAA Division I level for Iowa State. He just didn't have a lot of wins to show for it. After one season under Jackson, and without Sanderson, Jensen had a decision to make.

"I only wrestled for Kevin Jackson for one season," Jensen said. "I was willing to give Jackson a shot and I learned a lot. It just wasn't the right fit for me. I saw the direction the program was heading.

"I gave it a shot after Cael left. I loved Iowa State. I loved the school. I met my wife, Brenda, there. We met my freshman year in February. She finished her degree the following year at Iowa State."

Jensen reached out to Nebraska-Kearney coach Marc Bauer following that season.

"I was thinking about quitting wrestling, but I talked to Brenda about it and she said I needed to go transfer and finish my career. That turned out to be a really important decision," he said. "I had gone on a recruiting visit to UNK when I was in high school. I liked Coach Bauer, and I liked the school and I liked the program. After I called Bauer to tell him I was going to Iowa State, he told me the door is always open if anything happens."

Something happened and Jensen had a chance to become a starter right away for Nebraska-Kearney, a top program that had won the team title at the 2008 NCAA Division II Championships.

"I jumped right into the lineup at 141 pounds for UNK. I had a pretty good year," Jensen said. "I lost to Mario Morgan of Nebraska-Omaha in the national finals in 2011. I really enjoyed that season. It was a blast. It got me back to loving wrestling again."

Bauer was the perfect fit as Jensen's new head coach.

"Marc Bauer did a great job as the head coach," Jensen said. "I lost a match early in the season, and I was upset. Marc talked to me about the process and said he needed me to peak in March and not in December. He settled me down and put everything in perspective.

"Marc really cared about me outside of what I did on the wrestling mat. That really helped mold me into a coach. He had such a positive attitude and approach. That was exactly what I needed at the time as a 21-year-old. It was the perfect fit. Bauer helped re-energize me. He really played a big role putting me back on the right path."

Jensen came back the following season as the top returning national qualifier at 141. He was ranked No. 1 in NCAA DII at his weight class. He was still ranked No. 1 going into his final collegiate competition, the 2012 NCAA tournament in Pueblo, Colorado.

Jensen powered into the national finals for the second straight season, only the outcome was different this time around. He wasn't going to be a denied as a senior.

Jensen took command early, locking B.J. Young of Newberry in a cradle in the second period. Like he had so many times in his career, Jensen wasn't about to loosen his grip. He planted Young on his back, the referee slapped the mat and Jensen recorded a fall.

He had captured a national championship. It was a fitting end to a fabulous two years as a wrestler at Nebraska-Kearney for Jensen.

"I was pretty excited," Jensen said. "I was doing everything for the last time. It was my no regrets year. This was going to be it. I had a long career, going all the way back to when I was a little kid. I loved wrestling, but

I was ready to be done wrestling. The national title was one last thing I needed to do.

"Before the finals, I obviously knew it was going to be my last match. It was a relief to finish with a national title. It was a great way to finish. I felt like I had put a lot into it. The sport left me on a high note. We won a team title as well. I won an individual national title and a team national title. Something that was incredible and rare. I couldn't have scripted it much better. I was very blessed and fortunate to have it fall my way."

Jensen graduated shortly after that, in May 2012. He and Brenda were married that same month. She had moved to Kearney and worked while Jensen finished his degree during the 2011-12 school year.

He earned a degree in business administration with an emphasis in management.

Jensen was done competing, but he wasn't done with the Nebraska-Kearney wrestling program. At the end of Jensen's senior year, UNK head assistant coach Ty Swarm took over as the head coach at Kearney High School.

Bauer offered Jensen the assistant coaching position and he accepted. Jensen started coaching at UNK in the fall of 2012. He also started graduate school and earned his master's degree in business administration in the spring of 2014.

In Jensen's first year as an assistant coach, the Lopers struck gold again. UNK repeated as national champions, winning the Division II team title in 2013. It was the school's third championship in six seasons.

"My first year as a coach, we transitioned into being a really good team again," Jensen said. "We lost a bunch of guys from my senior year, but we had some athletes step up the following season.

"We pulled in some transfers. Daniel DeShazer and Romero Cotton came in after being at the Division I level. Raufeon Stots was a senior in 2013.

"It was a fun experience those couple of years," Jensen said. "It was pretty special to cap my career with a national title and a team title. And then jump into the coaching role and repeat the process. It makes you appreciate it even more."

It had taken some time, but Bauer had built Nebraska-Kearney into a national powerhouse.

"Marc was driven to challenge himself – I learned so much by watching and observing how he ran the wrestling program," Jensen said. "I was trying to learn as much as I could because I knew he wanted me to take over the program eventually.

"Coaching is a different role. All of a sudden, you don't have a lot of control over what happens. The athletes have to go out there and perform. You can guide them, teach them and encourage them, but it all comes down to the athletes. They have to perform."

In the summer of 2016, Bauer made the decision they knew was coming. After four years as an assistant coach, Jensen was promoted to the head coaching position at the University of Nebraska at Kearney. Jensen was just 27 years old and became one of the youngest college head coaches in the country.

"Marc had an opportunity to get his doctorate and teach in the exercise science department on campus. He decided to jump on that opportunity," Jensen said. "Marc told me, 'I want you to take over this program and I want to help you.' Marc has no ego in anything he does. That's what makes him such a good leader."

Jensen brought in Andrew Sorensen as his top assistant coach. They were teammates at Iowa State.

"Coach Bauer gave me some great advice," Jensen said. "He said, 'It is yours now. The blueprint is here to run a successful program. Athletics is changing and the sport is changing. You have all the characteristics to be a great coach, but make it your own.'

"Marc stuck around to help, but he let me run the show. He let me be the head coach. He was there to answer questions and provide guidance."

Jensen's first season as head coach brought more success to the UNK program. The Lopers finished fourth in the 2017 team standings at the NCAA tournament in Birmingham, Alabama.

"There was definitely a transition," Jensen said. "It is like any supervisor role. You don't know what they are dealing with until you step into the position. At the end of the day, we are not rocket scientists. We are wrestling coaches. It is a matter of how much time and effort that goes into it. It's as hard as you want to make it.

"We hold our program to a high standard. We want to stay engaged with our alumni with fundraising. And we want to win."

Jensen said he was excited for the opportunity to take

over a program that he had fallen in love with.

"It was like a dream come true," he said in 2023. "This was my dream job. I had the perspective of competing at a great Division I program and a great Division II program. I am also very in-tune with a good work-life balance. I love wrestling but I also want to have a great home life with my family.

"I don't have any goals or desires to coach at the Division I level. I love where I am at. I am at a great institution and Kearney is an amazing community. This program is top-notch and it is a great place to be. I don't see myself going anywhere."

Jensen's wife works as the city manager for Kearney, a community of 35,000 residents located in central Nebraska.

"My wife is awesome – she's done really well in her career," Jensen said. "She is very supportive of what I do. She met me as a freshman in college, so she knows what wrestling is like. She has been around it for a number of years."

The Jensens also expanded their family on October 25, 2022, when their son, Kellan Ames, entered the world.

"I am a dad now, and that changes everything," Dalton said. "When the season is over, I get our son ready and take him to day care. I also pick him up at the end of the day. It's rewarding. Kellan is awesome. It's been great seeing him grow. I love being a father."

Jensen has found the perfect balance between family and coaching.

"Nothing has changed about my passion for wrestling

and passion for coaching my guys," he said. "I love seeing my son when he wakes up in the morning. It really enhances my life. It gives you more perspective. I am up early to get him ready, and then I am here at the office by 8 a.m. every day."

Hall of Fame coach Tom McCann, the long-time head coach at Kearney High School, also joined the UNK staff as an assistant coach. Bauer wrestled for McCann at the high school level.

"Tom has years and years of wisdom," Jensen said. "It's great having him around. He is so knowledgeable, and he's just such a great man. He has really helped the program at UNK."

CHAPTER 9
PREVAILING IN PUEBLO

The 2011-12 wrestling season was one to remember for the Nebraska-Kearney Lopers. It also brought a significant change to the NCAA Division II landscape. Nebraska-Omaha had won the last three DII national titles. But just a few hours after winning the 2011 NCAA title in Kearney, UNO coach Mike Denney was informed by athletic director Trev Alberts that the wrestling program would be dropped.

Denney was UNK coach Marc Bauer's college coach and he also served as a mentor for him. It was shocking news to say the least. Bauer had maintained a close relationship with Denney over the years while they coached against each other.

While Denney was quickly hired as the first head coach at Maryville University in St. Louis, a number of Nebraska-Omaha wrestlers were looking for new homes. And two of them wound up in Kearney. Mark Fiala and Kevin Barrett were transfers from UNO who would play key roles on a Loper team that would go on to capture a national championship in 2012. Nebraska-Kearney edged St. Cloud State in a close team race, 107 points to 95, to capture the school's second NCAA title in wrestling.

"UNO probably would have won the national title the next two years – they were really loaded and they were in the driver's seat," Bauer said. "It was unfortunate what happened with their program. Coach Denney had done such an amazing job in Omaha.

"It changed everything for us when UNO dropped wrestling. We ended up with Barrett and Fiala. Without those two guys, we would not have won the national championship in 2012."

The 2012 national tournament was originally scheduled to be held in Cedar Rapids, Iowa, where the Lopers won their first title in 2008. But Cedar Rapids had issues with flooding, and the NCAA moved the tournament to Pueblo, Colorado.

The national tournament figured to be a close race between UNK and St. Cloud State, whose head coach was Bauer's college teammate and good friend Steve Costanzo.

The Lopers had a loaded lineup that was hitting their peak entering nationals.

"That was a pretty special team – we had three studs who were right in a row in our lineup," Bauer said. "And all three of them won national titles."

Senior Dalton Jensen, who finished second in the nation in 2011, led the way for the Lopers. Jensen powered into the finals before pinning B. J. Young of Newberry in the 141-pound finals. Jensen had an outstanding two seasons for Nebraska-Kearney after transferring in from Iowa State University.

"Dalton was second in 2011, and we knew he would come back with a vengeance the following season," Bauer said. "His technique is impeccable. He's long, lanky and hard to score on. And he was so good in the front headlock position. He could cradle guys and pin them in the blink of an eye."

Junior Raufeon Stots followed suit by capturing a national title for UNK at 149 pounds. Stots stormed into the title bout before earning a 5-4 victory over Maryville freshman Keenan Hagerty in the finals.

"Stots was pretty tough – he came through in some big matches," Bauer said. "He overcame some adversity and some injuries. And he wrestled his best at the national tournament."

The parade of Nebraska-Kearney champions continued with a third consecutive title at 157 pounds. Senior T.J. Hepburn pinned West Liberty senior Jarrod Shaw to capture a national championship.

"Hepburn was the best athlete I have ever coached," Bauer said. "T.J. was Division I caliber. We were really fortunate to have him in our lineup. He had a great performance that year at nationals."

Having three national champions in succession made for some interesting matchups during UNK practices.

"As you can imagine, we had some great battles in the wrestling room with those three," Bauer said. "They all pushed each other and made each other better. It was fun to watch those guys matching up in the room."

Loper senior Ross Brunkhardt came back from a semifinal setback to place third at 184 pounds. He capped his career with a 4-2 win over Central Oklahoma's Tanner Keck in the third-place bout.

UNK senior Joey Wilson turned in a strong performance to finish fourth at 165 pounds. Fiala won a pair of matches before placing eighth at 174 pounds.

"We had three champions, but we almost had five in the finals that year," Bauer said. "Brunkhardt and Wilson almost won their semifinal matches. They both lost by one point in the semis."

Barrett, whose brother Shaq went on to excel in the National Football League, also had a superb tournament. He finished fourth at heavyweight. Barrett won his first two matches before falling to eventual champion Matt Meuleners of Northern State in the semifinal round. Barrett won his next match by fall before dropping a 1-0 decision to Ashland's Jacob Southwick in the third-place match.

The Lopers finished with seven All-Americans, including three national champions, on a memorable weekend in Colorado.

"It was another great team effort in 2012," Bauer said. "It took a lot of guys and we needed to score a lot of points. We had a number of guys really step up and come through. It is always special when you win a national title and this team did an amazing job."

And more success was about to follow for the Nebraska-Kearney wrestling program.

CHAPTER 10
ACHIEVING HIS DREAM

Raufeon Stots grew up in Houston, Texas with his mother and two brothers. He didn't start competing in the sport of wrestling until his junior year at Klein Oak High School.

"My mom passed away my sophomore year in high school," Stots said. "She had health complications and pneumonia in her lungs. She was basically a single mom. My father paid child support, but he had moved away. My mom was on disability. Our money was tight and we were pinching pennies. I was really young when she died.

"She was a church-going woman. She made sure I took care of my grades. Doing well in school was a big priority and I was an honor student. She was super supportive. We were very close. She was pretty much our everything."

When his mother died, everything changed for Stots. And not for the better.

"After she passed, it was really difficult," he said. "We knew her health wasn't good, but when she passed it was still pretty devastating and heartbreaking. I feel like it changed my demeanor and it changed my view of the world. It was pretty terrible. I stopped doing homework and stopped going to classes."

Stots started living with an aunt, who was granted legal guardianship of him.

"She lived in a different part of Houston than where I was," he said. "I was commuting 40 minutes away to my high school. I was pretty much on my own. We had government assistance and would get a check for support. We would use it for food and gas. I had a place to stay and I appreciate my aunt for letting me stay there. But money was pretty scarce.

"I maintained a relationship with my father, and I still do, but I didn't see him much when I was growing up."

A turning point for Stots came when his science teacher, Brad Ewing, said he would give him a quiz point if he would give wrestling a try. Ewing was also the school's wrestling coach. He had competed in the sport at Nebraska-Kearney.

Stots was already a well-established football player. He played halfback and outside linebacker, starting on the varsity his junior season.

Following the football season, the 5-foot-6 Stots joined the wrestling team. He would compete at 145 pounds as a junior.

"Right away, I liked wrestling," he said. "I learned one move, a double leg takedown, when I first started. I had the speed and athleticism. That double leg was a technique I knew from tackling guys in football."

Stots said wrestling became a "great way to use some

pent-up frustration" after his mother had died.

"Wrestling became a great outlet for me," he said. "It was really good for me to have an activity I was focused on. And it was a tough, physical sport that was challenging. I really had to push myself to become good at it."

Stots competed on the junior varsity for two tournaments and won them both. His days on the JV squad were soon over. Stots earned a wrestle-off against the varsity starter and beat him. He had made the lineup.

"I didn't have any experience. I had never wrestled before, but I was a fast learner," he said.

Stots learned so quickly that he qualified for the 2006 Texas state tournament during his first season.

"But I didn't get to wrestle at state," he said. "Right before state, report cards came out. I was ineligible because of my grades. When that happened, it kind of set me straight. I started thinking about wrestling in college. I knew I had to take care of my grades. I realized I had to buckle down in the classroom. My coaches talked to me and encouraged me. After that, I started doing better in school."

Stots came back strong his senior season of high school and qualified for the 2007 state tournament.

"I lost a heartbreaker in the semifinals, and then I lost two more matches and got sixth," he said. "It was pretty disappointing, but it was also a good learning experience. After I lost in the semis, I wanted to go home. I didn't care about those last two matches. My goal was to win state. It was heartbreaking when it didn't happen."

Stots continued to wrestle over the summer months, competing in Greco-Roman and freestyle tournaments.

"That really helped me," he said. "I was still pretty green and inexperienced. I ended up getting a lot of matches in."

Stots won the Greco state title and placed second in freestyle in 2007. And he competed in the Junior Duals against top teams from around the country.

Stots wanted to keep wrestling and received an opportunity at Labette (Kansas) Community College. Joe Renfro, who had wrestled at Nebraska-Kearney, was the head coach at Labette.

"My high school coach knew the coach at Labette, and I went there for a recruiting trip," Stots said. "I went from Houston, Texas, the fourth biggest city in America, to a small town in Kansas. It was a pretty big transition."

Stots spent three years at Labette. He redshirted his first season there. Stots then made a big impact during the 2008-09 season. He placed fourth at the national junior college tournament. Stots had high hopes for his sophomore season, but he tore the meniscus in his knee and finished one win short of placing at nationals.

Stots then followed in his high school and junior college coaches' footsteps and joined the wrestling program at the University of Nebraska at Kearney in 2010.

"T.J. Hepburn, who ended up being a national champion, was already there and I knew I would be able to train with him," Stots said. "They had a good program, and I liked the coaches and the wrestlers they had there."

Stots stepped on the mat for his first tournament at UNK in 2010 when disaster struck.

"I dislocated my elbow in my first tournament," he said. "I was out for the season. I took a medical redshirt and still had two years of eligibility left in college."

Stots landed a spot in the Loper starting lineup at 149 pounds for the 2011-12 season.

"I started training with Dalton Jensen, who won a national title for UNK," Stots said. "I learned how to ride people. I was already pretty good on my feet, but working with Dalton helped me a lot. I was relying a lot on my athleticism, but I also learned how to wrestle down on the mat.

"Training with Dalton and T.J. Hepburn, we had some great battles. Joey Wilson was at 165, and he was a really good wrestler. Practice was tougher than the meets sometimes. That really helped me a lot, training with those guys in the room."

Stots qualified for the 2012 NCAA Division II tournament in Pueblo, Colorado. He entered the event with a 26-6 record at 149 pounds.

"I remember going in there feeling confident," he said. "I also felt really confident in our team. Everyone was firing on all cylinders. Marc Bauer does a good job of getting guys to peak at the right time. That was a great group of guys. We all rooted for each other. Dalton and T.J. were winning, and we all fed off that. I was right in the middle of those guys who were dominant."

Stots advanced to the national title match against surprise finalist Keegan Hagerty, an unranked wrestler at first-year program Maryville (Missouri).

"Hagerty was a freshman, and I figured I would take it to him because he was a young kid," Stots said. "It ended up being a tough match. I got a couple of early takedowns and I won 5-4."

Time ran out and Stots won a season-ending tournament for the first time.

"I just remember being the happiest I had ever been," he said. "I had come a long way to reach that goal and become a national champion. That was the biggest deep breath I had ever taken. It also helped us win a team title. That was icing on the cake. It couldn't get any better. That was the best day ever. That first one was special. I set a goal to do it, but when you attain it, that is pretty amazing. It was crazy. And it was awesome."

Stots came back the following season and reached the finals at the 2013 national tournament in Birmingham, Alabama.

"That year was even more fun for me," he said.

"I was one of the leaders on the team. We had another excellent team. I knew what to expect and how to approach it. It was super special."

Stots downed Jacob Horn of St. Cloud State 4-3 in the finals. He had won his second national championship.

"Horn was really good at riding and turning people. He was crazy good on top," Stots said. "I felt like I was wrestling my best in that tournament. That was more expected, but I was still very happy when I won it. I was still going out on top. We won the team championship again. I decided to do a dance after I won. They deducted a team point. They thought I had taunted my opponent, but I was just excited I had won back-to-back national titles. It was an amazing moment. I'll never forget it."

Stots has gone on to excel in mixed martial arts. He was Bellator's interim world champion.

"My background in wrestling helps me so much in MMA," he said. "The work ethic translated really well to mixed martial arts. I developed a winning mindset in wrestling and that has carried over. I learned how to show up at the gym and work hard. You've got to put the time and effort into it.

"Wrestling taught me a lot of good life lessons. It has taken me to some great places."

Stots is back living in Houston. He and his wife, Michaela, who played volleyball at UNK, have two sons. Their boys, Clarence and Ikechukwu, turned 6 and 3 in 2024.

Stots reflects fondly on his days at Nebraska-Kearney.

"It was a great experience at UNK," he said. "It was the perfect place for me. Marc Bauer did a good job developing wrestlers along with good family men and citizens. I grew up a lot when I was there. And I met my wife there – she is the love of my life and my kids' mother. I am proud to be a part of the UNK wrestling program. I have come a long way in my life and the time I spent in Kearney, Nebraska played a big part in that."

CHAPTER 11
BACK-TO-BACK

The 2013 NCAA Division II Championships figured to be another close battle for the team title. Returning champion Nebraska-Kearney was the favorite while St. Cloud State and Notre Dame College also brought strong teams to the national tournament in Birmingham, Alabama.

As expected, the tournament came right down to the wire. Coach Marc Bauer and the UNK Lopers repeated as champions with 108 points. Nebraska-Kearney won its third national team title. St. Cloud State was a close second with 105 points and Notre Dame College was third with 103.5 points.

"The 2012 and 2013 teams were much different," Bauer said. "We lost a lot of seniors from the 2012 team and we had a lot of new faces in our lineup. We had our share of challenges that year as we were trying to figure everything out. That was a really hard year for me with so many changes."

The 2012 and 2013 teams were different, but there were similarities as well.

"The 2013 team had some major horsepower, even more than the year before because of some transfers," Bauer said. "We had some talented kids on that team, that's for sure. I felt like we were going to win the tournament that year. We had some really good wrestlers on that team."

Nebraska-Kearney pushed four wrestlers into the finals and crowned a pair of champions. Freshman Daniel DeShazer captured the 133-pound national title and teammate Raufeon Stots repeated as national champion at 149 pounds.

DeShazer stormed into the finals for a matchup against St. Cloud State's Andy Pokorny, a transfer from the University of Nebraska. DeShazer prevailed in a close bout, earning a 7-5 victory to win a national championship.

Stots followed by coming through again in the finals. He earned a hard-fought 4-3 win over St. Cloud State's Jacob Horn in the title bout.

The UNK victories by Stots and DeShazer were pivotal as the Lopers held off St. Cloud State for the team championship.

"They both beat St. Cloud State wrestlers in the finals – and that obviously was huge for us," Bauer said. "Stots won finals matches in 2012 and 2013 that solidified the tournament outcome. He really came through for us."

Nebraska-Kearney also had two wrestlers who placed second that season.

Senior Chase Nelson, a transfer from Oklahoma,

advanced to the 165-pound finals before falling 7-5 to Joey Davis of Notre Dame. Davis, a freshman, would go on to win four national titles in Division II.

Loper Romero Cotton won three bouts to reach the title bout at 197 pounds. Cotton was locked in a tight battle with Maryville's Matt Baker in the finals and the bout went into overtime. Baker eventually earned a 5-4 victory.

"That was a great match between very good wrestlers," Bauer said.

Cotton, a transfer from the University of Nebraska, would go on to have one of the best careers in Nebraska-Kearney history. He made the finals three more times in his Loper career and became a three-time national champion.

Cotton excelled in wrestling despite competing only in the second half of the season during his four years of eligibility at UNK. Cotton spent the fall semesters playing football for the Lopers.

"Romero played football all four years at UNK. And he was a three-national champion. That's pretty darn impressive," Bauer said. "He always played football and then didn't join the wrestling team until late December. It would take him a while to get into wrestling shape, but he was always at his best at the national tournament.

"When the bright lights were on, Romero would shine bright. He was a heck of an athlete. He only wrestled four semesters in college, but he had a heck of a career for us."

Cotton also was an athlete who fit in well with the

tight-knit Loper wrestling family.

"Romero is an outstanding young man," Bauer said. "He was great to work with. I really enjoyed coaching him. He obviously meant a tremendous amount to our wrestling program."

The Lopers also had 2013 All-Americans in Chase White at 157 pounds and Patrick Martinez at 174 pounds. Both wrestlers placed fifth at nationals.

Martinez, a transfer from Wyoming, would go on to make the U.S. World Team in Greco-Roman wrestling.

"It is always special when you win," Bauer said. "We had won our third national title as a team, but we had won a lot of other trophies over the years. It takes a lot of people to make something special happen. It also takes family and alumni. There are so many factors that go into it."

Bauer had been thinking about stepping aside as Nebraska-Kearney head coach following the 2012-13 season.

"I was ready to be done in 2013 and didn't quit until 2016," he said. "When Dalton Jensen graduated, I was thinking about 'what's next?' And I was thinking Dalton could be our next head coach. He's super intelligent, he's a great leader, he has strong character and integrity. He's a wonderful person. I was looking down the road for a successor and I knew he was that person. I started grooming him to be my successor. Dalton was an assistant coach for me and I knew it was going to happen, and it did in 2016. I stepped aside and he became the head coach at the University of Nebraska at Kearney."

Bauer and the UNK program had come a long way since he took over the program nearly two decades before.

"We've had alumni from way back in our early days who have continued to support the program. That's really important for the success. We have had amazing support," Bauer said. "The success our program has had, it makes me proud to see what we've done. When we won our third title, I reflected about what all went into that. It had taken an awful lot to get there. It was a pretty amazing transformation."

The Loper program also had opportunities to experience other cultures.

"Every four years, we would try to go on a trip," Bauer said. "We went to Bulgaria, Germany and China. Dalton took the team to Greece. Those trips are fun. You experience so much and it is a great opportunity for the team to bond."

Bauer also had a chance to travel abroad when Dlagnev wrestled for the United States at the 2012 and 2016 Olympic Games.

"I went to London and Rio de Janeiro to see Tervel wrestle at the Olympics," Bauer said.

During the 2016 Olympics in Brazil, Bauer had a chance to hang out with his old college coach.

"My wife and I hung out with Coach Denney and his wife, Bonnie," Bauer said. "George Ivanov, who wrestled for Coach Denney at UNO, was wrestling in the Olympics for Bulgaria. We went to Christ the Redeemer with Coach Denney and Bonnie. It was a great trip.

"It was a once in a lifetime thing to have Tervel

wrestling in the Olympics and then have Marty Usman win the UFC. It was pretty incredible," he said. "But we've had so many young men who have gone on to excel in their lives. It's really neat to see. The Nebraska-Kearney wrestling program, it is a family. And it's been great to have been a part of it."

CHAPTER 12
'ONE BIG FAMILY'

Wrestlers from the DeShazer family experienced an enormous amount of success in the state of Kansas. Daniel DeShazer Sr. won two state titles before going on to wrestle at Labette Community College and the University of Dubuque. His older son Tristen captured four state titles before wrestling collegiately for Northern Illinois University.

Daniel DeShazer Jr. then followed in his father's and brother's footsteps. He grew up in Wichita and won three state championships for Wichita Heights High School.

"My dad was our family's first state champion and my brother was the first African American to win four state titles in Kansas," Daniel Jr. said. "Wrestling obviously was a very big deal in our family. It really bonded us and brought us together."

Daniel DeShazer Jr. had high hopes coming out of high school. He joined high school teammate Kendric Maple at the University of Oklahoma. Maple would go on to win an NCAA title for the Sooners.

"(World champion and Olympic silver medalist)

Sammie Henson recruited me to OU," DeShazer said. "And Kendric Maple was already there. It looked like a good fit for me."

DeShazer redshirted his first year at Oklahoma. He ended up having shoulder surgery and also had issues off the mat.

"I got into a little bit of trouble," he said. "We got into a scuffle, and I ended up losing my scholarship."

DeShazer was looking to transfer to another NCAA Division I school.

"I was going to go to Oklahoma State," he said. "I had enrolled there, but then it didn't seem like the right fit."

DeShazer also had been talking with the University of Nebraska at Kearney.

"UNK offered me a full scholarship," he said. "And Chase Nelson, who went to high school and to Oklahoma with me, was already at UNK. Plus, Raufeon Stots, another really good wrestler, was already there."

DeShazer headed to Nebraska-Kearney in the summer of 2012.

"UNK had just won the national title and they had a lot of guys that were returning," he said.

DeShazer also had another reason for transferring to the NCAA Division II school.

"I played football in high school, and I was second team all-state," he said. "One of the reasons I went to UNK was to play football. I wanted to play two sports there."

Before he played football in college, DeShazer

joined the Loper wrestling team for the 2012-13 season. He went 31-8 and captured an NCAA DII title at 133 pounds in Birmingham, Alabama.

DeShazer was in a loaded bracket that included two-time national champion Trevor Franklin of Upper Iowa and returning national runner-up Andy Pokorny of St. Cloud State.

DeShazer won by fall in the semifinals to land a berth in the finals against Pokorny, who had been a starter for one season at the University of Nebraska.

"Once I got to the finals, it was very electric," DeShazer said. "It was a tight team race with St. Cloud State. We had put four guys in the finals and we were rolling."

DeShazer was locked in a tight bout against Pokorny before prevailing 7-5. DeShazer had captured a national title as a freshman.

"That finals match was huge for me," DeShazer said. "I was a freshman, but I went into that tournament with a chip on my shoulder. I had something to prove. There were some returning finalists that were expected to do well, and that motivated me. I had to seal the deal."

DeShazer was confident when he walked onto the mat for the national championship bout.

"No way I was losing that match," he said. "I controlled the pace. I hit three duck unders and a double leg. I really wanted it."

When time ran out, his hand was raised by the official and it was time to celebrate.

"Oh man, I started dancing a little bit. It felt really

good," DeShazer said. "It's tough to win a national tournament. The team race was on the line. Winning that team title was amazing. It is the best wrestling memory I've ever had."

DeShazer's goal of winning four national titles was still intact, but he also had another goal.

"I joined the football team later that year in 2013," he said. "I was a running back. It went pretty well. I was only 5-4 and 150 pounds, but I was used to being one of the smallest guys on the field.

"I knew I was going to work hard. Romero Cotton, who was one of our best wrestlers, also was a running back on the team."

There were doubters and skeptics when DeShazer joined the Loper football team, but he proved them wrong.

"I learned the playbook and worked my way up the depth chart," he said. "I played a little bit the first game and played some more the second game. By the third game, I was starting. I carried the ball and caught it. I just outworked everybody. I had a lot of speed and could get myself open.

"I started four games before I tore some ligaments in my ankle. I didn't play much after that. But it was a good experience and I am glad I played in college. That ended up being the end of my football career."

The ankle injury carried over into DeShazer's sophomore year of wrestling.

He finished 17-3 before placing second at the national tournament in 2014. He also earned all-academic honors.

"The ankle bothered me, but by nationals I was good to go," DeShazer said.

DeShazer advanced to the championship bout for the second straight year and squared off against Central Oklahoma's Casey Rowell in the finals.

DeShazer had defeated Rowell at the 2013 national tournament, but this match turned out differently. The match was tied 1-1 after regulation and went into overtime.

"He got me back," DeShazer said. "He won it with riding time. It was terrible. I had never lost like that. He had a good game plan and shut down my offense. It was a little devastating, especially the way I lost."

DeShazer came back stronger and more determined after the setback in the national finals.

"I was more motivated than ever," he said. "There was no more football. All my focus was on wrestling after that. I was ready to go."

It was a tough road again at the 2015 national tournament. DeShazer edged Nate Rodriguez of Ouachita Baptist 2-1 in overtime in the semifinals. He followed by downing Ashland's Michael Labry 7-6 in overtime to win his second national title.

"I had wrestled Labry in freestyle the previous summer and he beat me at a tournament," DeShazer said. "It was another tight match, but I was able to come out on top. It felt good. It didn't feel like the first one, but I was back on top of the throne where I was supposed to be. Me and Romero Cotton won it that year. Winning it with

Romero, one of my childhood friends, was an amazing feeling."

DeShazer came back determined to win his third national title in 2016.

"Things were going good," he said. "I was wrestling well. I was beating a lot of top Division I guys."

But DeShazer ran into a tough semifinal opponent at the NCAA Championships. He dropped a close match to Pitt-Johnstown's Nick Roberts, a transfer from Ohio State.

"He stayed in good position, and I lost 2-1," DeShazer said. "He scored an early penalty point and that was the difference in the match. I bounced back, winning my last two matches to take third. I was trying to score bonus points to help our team. Romero won it again and Destin McCauley won it for UNK."

DeShazer finished as a four-time NCAA Division II All-American after placing first, second, first and third at the national tournament.

"It didn't finish quite the way I had hoped, but I had some good success and our team did really well," he said.

DeShazer has continued to wrestle at the Senior level while competing in freestyle. He made the U.S. National Team at 61 kg/134 pounds in 2022. He was ranked No. 3 in the country at his weight class.

DeShazer's days at UNK paved the way for him to excel against Olympic level athletes. He has fond memories from his time at Nebraska-Kearney.

"The UNK experience was amazing," he said. "I wouldn't call what we had a team, it was more of a family. We were really tight-knit at Nebraska-Kearney. I loved my time there. It was definitely a great experience to be part of a legendary program. We had great coaches and I had great teammates. It was one big family in a little town in the middle of Nebraska. My time at UNK holds a special place in my heart that will always be there."

CHAPTER 13
COTTON'S EXCLUSIVE CLUB

R omero Cotton accomplished about as much as an athlete possibly could at the prep level. He had an outstanding four-year career at Hutchinson (Kansas) High School.

Cotton was a four-time state champion in wrestling. He also played on four state championship teams in football and was a two-time all-state running back.

Cotton excelled against the country's best competition, capturing USA Wrestling Cadet National championships in freestyle and Greco-Roman in 2006. He also was a two-time powerlifting state champion during his prep days.

As you can imagine, Cotton became a major target of top NCAA Division I schools. He eventually signed with the University of Nebraska.

"I was going to try to play football and wrestle at Nebraska," Cotton said. "My recruiting trip was awesome. My hosts were Jordan Burroughs and Vince Jones, who went on to great careers in wrestling. Jordan went on to win the Olympics (in 2012)."

Two days before Cotton arrived in Lincoln in 2008,

he was arrested. He faced assault charges after an altercation in Kansas.

Cotton redshirted for the University of Nebraska wrestling team during the 2008-09 school year. He placed second in one of the first open tournaments he competed in.

Cotton was still facing assault charges in the fall of 2009 when his life changed.

"I signed a plea agreement and I thought I was going to get probation," he said. "My lawyer was talking about seven to 13 months of probation and no jail time."

But that didn't happen. Cotton was convicted of aggravated battery and sentenced to 38 months in prison. He spent time in three different facilities in Kansas. He served 30 months of his sentence before being granted an early release.

"It was horrible being in prison – it was awful," Cotton said. "I wasn't expecting that and I wasn't ready for it. It was pretty devastating when I found out I was going to prison."

Cotton said he had plenty of time to think while he was incarcerated.

"It was extremely boring and it was a little scary at times," he said. "I was 19 years old when I was sentenced to prison. I was really young, but I had a lot of people looking out for me when I was in there. A lot of people took care of me during my time in prison. I was very lucky to have good people with me when I was in there."

Cotton figured his athletic career was over.

"At the beginning, when I first went to prison, I

didn't think anybody was going to want me when I got out," he said. "I was thinking I was done competing. I was going to be too old and I didn't think anyone would want me after the trouble I had gotten into."

While Cotton was in prison, numerous people encouraged him to think about competing in college athletics again after he was released.

"I wanted to compete again, but I didn't know if I could," he said. "I had put on some weight. I was around 240 pounds. I was lifting weights, but a lot of the food we were eating in prison wasn't all that healthy. Toward the end of my sentence, I started thinking about going back to school. My dad always wanted me to get a college degree.

"My parents and my girlfriend were super supportive when I was in prison. I had friends that were also supportive and a lot of people wrote me letters. I never really lost contact with anybody that was close to me."

Cotton entered prison in September 2009 and was released in April 2012. He was 22 years old when he walked out as a free man.

"It was really a difficult time obviously," he said. "But I was determined to come back out and have a good life."

Cotton initially couldn't leave the state of Kansas because he was on parole. He briefly went to Fort Hays State, but he learned he was ineligible.

Cotton then started looking at other options. He learned that Daniel DeShazer and Chase Nelson, two wrestlers he had grown up with in Kansas, had left the University of Oklahoma. They had both transferred to the

University of Nebraska at Kearney, an NCAA Division II school.

"I had no idea where Kearney was," Cotton said. "Those guys gave me a good recommendation for UNK. And my parole officer signed off where I could now leave the state."

Cotton visited Nebraska-Kearney and liked what he saw.

"Coach Bauer was cool – he was great and the guys on the team liked him," he said. "Plus, my homies were there. And they said I could play football and wrestle."

Cotton headed to UNK and started taking classes.

"I was ineligible when I first got to UNK," he said. "But I eventually got a waiver that I was eligible right before the regional tournament in 2013."

Cotton hadn't been on the wrestling mat in four years.

"It was terrible when I first went into the room and started training," he said. "I came down from 220 pounds to 197. I didn't cut my weight very well.

"I went to my first college tournament and I got beat up pretty good. I wasn't moving my feet very well. And I was gassed – I wasn't in very good shape yet. I wrestled against a guy from Wyoming who was really good and he really took it to me. It took a while for me to make it back to where I had been. I had no clue how I was going to do in that season."

Cotton came on strong in the second half of the 2012-13 season. He qualified for the NCAA Division II Championships and won his first two matches to reach the semifinals.

And then he came back the next day with a win to qualify for the finals. He would face Matt Baker of Maryville for the 197-pound national title.

The match with Baker was close and hard-fought. Baker, also from Kansas, was able to prevail over Cotton in overtime.

"That was a tough match against a good kid," Cotton said. "I finished second in the nation after four years away from the sport. We won the team title and I still got a ring. All things considered, it was a pretty good season."

A week later, Cotton was playing football. He joined the Lopers for spring practice. Cotton ended up excelling for the UNK football team. He rushed for more than 1,500 career yards in college while earning all-conference honors at running back for the Lopers.

"It was a lot of fun playing football," he said. "It was great to get in there and play. I never imagined being able to play both sports again after everything I went through."

Cotton rejoined the wrestling team for the 2013-14 season and was ranked No. 1 nationally all season. He went 21-0 that winter against Division II competition.

Cotton advanced to the finals of the NCAA DII Championships for the second straight season, He edged Julian Smith of McKendree 8-7 in the 197-pound national finals.

"I didn't know who Julian Smith was before the tournament, but he kept winning and ended up in the finals," Cotton said. "I was actually down by four or five points against him in the finals and had to come back. I eventually broke him and he gassed. I scored a few takedowns and won the match by one point. It was amazing to win it. I was behind and I came back to win it. To win like that, and become a national champion, it was super great."

Cotton started the 2014-15 wrestling season late again after playing football in the fall. He had another tough match in the finals of the 2015 NCAA DII meet in St. Louis. He defeated Huston Evans of Newberry 3-1 in sudden victory. Cotton won his second national title.

"He was a big strong dude," Cotton said. "He didn't move much and he slowed me down. I was able to take him down in overtime to win my second title. It was a great way to end the season. We didn't win the team title, but we still had a good season."

Cotton came back during the 2015-16 season looking to become Nebraska-Kearney's first three-time national champion. But before he made it to nationals, he lost at the regional tournament.

"I was sick between regionals and nationals," he said. "I wasn't feeling well at all and had lost some weight. Luckily, I had some time to get back on track before nationals."

Cotton advanced to the national finals for the fourth straight season. He downed Joe Gomez of Northern State 4-1 in his final collegiate match to become the first Loper to win three national titles.

"It was a tough season, but I finished the job," he said. "It was great to win my third title. I had a lot of great support from my coaches and teammates. They really pushed me and encouraged me. It was a great feeling to do that for our school."

Wrestling alongside DeShazer in college meant a great deal to Cotton. DeShazer also grew up in Kansas and won two national titles at UNK.

"Dap, that's my brother. I've known Daniel since he was 3 years old and I wrestled with his older brother as well," Cotton said. "I grew up with Dap and Chase Nelson. We are all still real tight. It was great being teammates with them in college."

DeShazer also enjoyed being on the same Loper teams with Cotton.

"Romero is one of the best athletes I have ever seen," DeShazer said. "He was in our kids' club in Kansas growing up. He had a great work ethic and mindset. He was going to get the job done. He was the second African American to win four state titles in Kansas. He overcame a lot of adversity. He had a great career playing football and wrestling at UNK. He is a great friend and he was an awesome teammate."

Cotton has gone on to excel in mixed martial arts. He has compiled a 6-2 record while fighting at 185 pounds. He has trained with past UFC champion Daniel Cormier, an Olympian and World medalist in wrestling. Cotton was living and training in San Jose, California in 2024.

None of it may have been possible if Cotton hadn't landed at the University of Nebraska at Kearney.

"I joined a great program with some great teammates that I really looked up to and learned from," he said. "My time at UNK was life altering. It changed my life and was transformational. I really got back on track when I went to Kearney, Nebraska. I'm still a Loper and I always will be. I'm still part of the wrestling family there. It's amazing to be a part of it."

CHAPTER 14
2022 CHAMPS

When Dalton Jensen moved to central Nebraska in 2010, he had high expectations. He had no idea what was about to transpire, but what a ride it has been for the Iowa native.

Jensen captured a national title at 141 pounds and was a member of an NCAA Division II championship team in 2012 for the University of Nebraska at Kearney.

A decade later, he became a championship coach at age 33. Jensen led the Lopers to an incredible performance at the 2022 NCAA Division II Championships in St. Louis.

UNK clinched the team title before the finals and rolled to the school's fourth NCAA crown at Chaifetz Arena.

The top-ranked Lopers powered to the team title with 127 points, the highest total in the event in 12 years. They delivered when it counted most, going a combined 15-7 in their matches on the final day.

"Our guys really stepped up to the plate," Jensen said. "They were motivated to come back after finishing a close second in 2021. Our guys were really focused from the start. We got a pin in the first match and we never lost the lead."

Second-ranked Central Oklahoma finished a distant second with 86 points. West Liberty was third with 75.5. Three-time defending champion St. Cloud State was fourth with 67 points.

Nebraska-Kearney captured its first national team title since going back-to-back in 2012 and 2013.

"We had a bunch of seniors come back after being granted the extra year because of Covid – they wanted to have a historical ending," Jensen said. "Their performance showed that. They wrestled their tails off. It was really impressive."

That list of Loper seniors was topped by Matt Malcom, who won the national title at 165 pounds. He beat Shane Gantz of UW-Parkside 1-0 in the finals.

"Matt was the backbone of this program for six years," Jensen said. "I can't think of anybody more deserving. He stayed focused, and he was one of the best pound-for-pound wrestlers in Division II. He wanted to win that team title for our program and his teammates."

The finals match wasn't quite what anyone expected, especially his head coach.

"That match was pretty uncharacteristic of Matt, who scored a lot of points," Jensen said. "He was the most dominant wrestler in Division II that year. Winning 1-0 wasn't his typical match. He had to win by relying on being savvy and trusting his wrestling IQ. He won in a tough battle."

Malcom made an immediate impact as a freshman for the Lopers. He became an All-American after placing fourth at the 2018 NCAA Division II Championships.

Malcom came back even stronger a year later, winning his final 20 matches of the season to capture his first national title at 157 pounds.

Malcom was all set to win his second national title in 2020 before the national tournament was cancelled because of the Covid-19 pandemic. He finished with a 30-8 record during the 2019-20 season.

Malcom placed fifth at nationals at 165 pounds in 2021 before winning a national title the following season.

"He had a lot to prove," Jensen said. "He was pretty determined to finish strong in his last season."

Malcom became Nebraska-Kearney's first five-time All-American.

"The team title was already clinched when Matt went out there for the national finals," Jensen said. "He was our last finalist of three. It was icing on the cake. He ended his career the way he deserved to. It was so satisfying. It was impressive to see him cap it with a championship."

Malcom had been joined in the national finals that season by senior teammates Josh Portillo (125) and Sam Turner (149), who both finished second for UNK.

"Portillo came back strong at the national tournament," Jensen said. "He provided a spark for us and he also scored a bunch of bonus points. He was really determined and it paid off for him."

Portillo was a transfer who had started his career at South Dakota State, an NCAA Division I school.

"I put a lot of hours into the recruitment of Portillo," Jensen said. "He wanted to wrestle there at a Division I school and he was at SDSU for a year and a half. His dad called me in October 2017 and told me Josh was looking at transferring. He was looking at four DI schools. It was a long process. He made his decision on Christmas Day."

"Josh called me and said, 'I'm ready to be a Loper.' I was anticipating and waiting for his call," Jensen said. "I was like a kid on Christmas morning when he gave me the news. I was excited. I knew what he was capable of."

Portillo, a three-time Iowa state champion from Clarion, came to Kearney during the middle of the season and jumped right into the Loper lineup.

"He wrestled at National Duals and he ended up being an All-American after placing fifth at nationals in 2018," Jensen said.

Jensen could identify with the wrestlers who had transferred to UNK after starting their careers at the Division I level.

"That was my journey – and that is what I had done in my own career," he said. "I can relate to what a lot of them are going through. It ended up working out really well for Josh."

Portillo placed second nationally in 2019 before missing the 2020 nationals after the event was cancelled.

He fell short of placing in 2021 before finishing second in the country again in 2022. Portillo was also an Academic All-American.

Turner was another wrestler who started his career at the DI level. He was a two-time NCAA qualifier for

Wyoming before looking to make a move. Turner came to Kearney in 2019.

"Sam jumped right in at 149 pounds and was an All-American," Jensen said.

Jensen landed those transfers after initially recruiting them when they were in high school.

"Those kids, I had already built those relationships," the coach said. "A lot of kids obviously are fixated on wrestling at the Division I level, and I understand that. I try to be objective about it as a coach. I understand what a high school senior is going through.

"I want kids with high expectations who want to reach the highest level. I am told no a lot. But there have been cases where I have kept the door open when things don't work out. That's what I did. It is the same way I continue to recruit."

Those transfers led the way on a loaded Loper team filled with excellent wrestlers.

The 2022 national championship team also saw Wesley Dawkins (133) and Billy Higgins (184) place third for the Lopers, Austin Eldredge (174) finish fourth, and Lee Herrington (285) and Nick James (141) take fifth.

Dawkins had previously placed second and fourth at nationals.

"Wesley Dawkins came back in 2022 and wrestled really well," Jensen said. "He scored a bunch of bonus points for us."

Higgins excelled for Nebraska prep powerhouse Omaha Skutt Catholic before starting his college career at

Northern Colorado at the DI level.

"Billy is an unbelievably talented athlete," Jensen said. "He really broke through in that tournament to finish third."

Eldredge came back to win a national title for Nebraska-Kearney at 174 pounds in 2023. He upset top seed and previously unbeaten Abner Romero of St. Cloud State 12-4 in the finals. That capped a 28-4 season for Eldredge.

"Of all the studs that have come through this program, Austin scored the most team points of any Loper," Jensen said. "He had two techs and two majors at 2023 nationals. He scored 24 team points. He had a major over the returning national champ from St. Cloud in the finals."

James and Herrington also came through for Nebraska-Kearney. Both wrestled at Kearney High School

"Nick had his best finish at nationals," Jensen said. "Lee was a workhorse and it paid off for him."

UNK had four All-Americans that season who were from the state of Nebraska, including the two from Kearney.

Jensen reflected on the season a few days after his team won the national title in 2022.

"I've been very blessed," Jensen said. "I have a lot of great support from Marc Bauer, our administration, our school, and our fans. We have had great young men wrestle for us. So much goes into this and I'm very grateful to be a part of it."

The heartbreak and disappointment of 2021 provided the fuel that boosted the Lopers to their magical run a year later.

"We were really determined," Jensen said. "We didn't know with 100 percent certainty who all would come back. Some guys were weighing whether they wanted to come back for another season. Six guys had the extra year and they all came back. Four of them were starters.

"I am not sure they all would have come back if we would have won it all in 2021. They all came back with a chip on their shoulders. That made it so extra special because of what we had endured and overcome to get to that 2022 title. It made our run feel even greater."

Missing out on the 2020 nationals because of Covid was even more heartbreaking. UNK was just hours away from competing at the national tournament in Sioux Falls, South Dakota when news came that the tournament was cancelled.

"That was really rough – we had never experienced anything like that before," Jensen said. "We were ranked third and we had another good team.

"We drove up there on Wednesday, and then on Thursday I went to the head coaches meeting. Everything seemed to be normal."

Then Jensen's phone dinged with the unfortunate news.

"I got a text from NCAA saying the tournament was called off," he said. "We were just about to have a team meeting before we were going to do our last workout.

When I got the text, it was mid-afternoon on Thursday with the tournament scheduled to start the next day."

Less than half an hour later, Jensen called a team meeting at their hotel.

"At that point, the guys did not know yet," the coach said. "I broke the news to them. They had no clue. I had to deliver the worst news possible. Obviously, it was very, very difficult."

Jensen said it was challenging to find the right words to tell his wrestlers that their biggest tournament of the season was cancelled. They were not going to be able to compete.

"Sometimes life isn't fair," Jensen told his wrestlers. "They cancelled the tournament. You guys aren't going to have an opportunity to chase that national title this year. There is nothing I can say to make it better."

The Loper wrestlers, similar to athletes from other schools in the same situation, were floored by the news.

"You could hear a pin drop in that room," Jensen said. "It was utter silence. We had one senior that year – Jarrod Hinrichs, our heavyweight who was second at nationals the year before. That was his last shot. He was ranked second and he had lost by one point in the finals the year before.

"Jarrod was the first one on my mind after I got that text. I went and gave him a big hug. I told him I loved him and I appreciated all that he did for the program. I felt so bad for Jarrod, and for all the guys on our team."

Jensen said it was an unforgettable day.

"I just wanted to console our guys," he said. "Then I

saw other teams going through the same thing in our hotel. It wasn't just us. It was a tough day for a lot of wrestlers around the country."

NCAA tournaments were also cancelled for athletes in Division I and Division III because of Covid.

"We gave the guys a couple of hours to process everything and then we took them out to eat," Jensen said. "Everyone was dealing with Covid. People were losing family members and people were dying. We were mad we lost our opportunity to wrestle at nationals, but there were a lot worse things happening. People were losing their lives and losing their livelihood. Our campus shut down and everything moved online.

"Our coaching staff and some of the wrestlers ended up delivering meals in Kearney to people in need. We just tried to make the best out of a difficult situation."

CHAPTER 15
FIVE-TIME ALL-AMERICAN

Matt Malcom figured he was done with school. And done with wrestling. Following a redshirt season at the University of Iowa during the 2016-17 school year, Malcom left Iowa City and he returned to his hometown. He had captured an Iowa state high school championship for Glenwood High School in 2016.

"I loved every minute of being a part of the wrestling program at Iowa," Malcom said. "But off the mat, I just wasn't happy. I had been a straight A student, but I was really struggling in school when I went to college. I wasn't happy with who I was.

"I went back home and was working some odd jobs over the summer. I wasn't planning on going back to school. And I really thought I was done with wrestling."

One person who believed Malcom wasn't done was Nebraska-Kearney coach Dalton Jensen. He had also grown up in southwest Iowa, near Omaha and close to where Malcom was from. Jensen called Malcom that July and they spoke on the phone.

"We talked for 15 minutes and the word wrestling never came up," Malcom said. "Dalton talked to me about life and family and school. I could tell right away that he truly had my back as a person and a student. We really connected on the phone. I owe a lot to Dalton."

A short time later, Malcom traveled to the University of Nebraska at Kearney campus for a visit. He met with Jensen and assistant coach Andrew Sorenson.

"I was really impressed with both of those guys," Malcom said. "You could see how genuine they were. And you could tell that they really care about their wrestlers. That made a big impact on me."

Malcom was sold. He was going to give college and the sport of wrestling another shot. He enrolled at the University of Nebraska at Kearney in the fall of 2017.

"I knew quite a bit about their program and that they had been successful," Malcom said. "I hit the ground running when I got there. I connected with my teammates right away, and I felt really comfortable. It was a good group of guys."

Malcom also was comfortable being back on the wrestling mat. He was all set to compete in his first match for the Lopers, but then those plans were put on hold.

"I found out that I was ineligible my first semester at UNK because of my grades when I was at Iowa," he said. "I didn't step on the mat to compete until the second semester in January."

Malcom made an immediate impact, landing a spot at the 2018 NCAA Division II Championships in Cedar Rapids, Iowa. He dropped his first match, but he rebounded to finish fourth in the nation at 157 pounds.

"I didn't have a lot of matches at the DII level and I was able to come back pretty well after losing in the first round," he said. "Overall, I didn't hang my head. I had a good season – it was something I could definitely build on."

Malcom carried the momentum over into his sophomore season. He powered into the finals of the 2019 national tournament in Cleveland before defeating surprise finalist Colin Ayers of Augustana 9-4 in the 157-pound title match. Malcom scored three takedowns and collected nearly three minutes of riding time in the victory.

"I was pretty confident going into the national tournament," he said. "I just tried to enjoy the moment when I made it to the finals. I knew all the work was done and I trusted that.

"I took my finals opponent down in the first 15 seconds and had a rideout in the first period. I controlled the match after that."

Malcom kept the pressure on en route to the victory. Time ran out and Malcom had captured a national title. Not bad for a guy who thought he was done wrestling less than two years before.

"I was happy and excited when I won – it was a sigh of relief," he said. "Everything I had done to prepare for that moment had paid off. After winning that first one, I knew I wanted to win two more.

"I wasn't completely satisfied. I wanted my teammates to enjoy the same feeling I did. I wasn't sad, but I wanted those guys to have success as well."

Malcom moved up to 165 pounds the following season and was expected to contend for another national title.

"I was ranked pretty high and I felt like I could win it," he said. "I was wrestling pretty well going into nationals."

When the Lopers arrived for the 2020 national tournament in Sioux Falls, South Dakota, Malcom was concerned. He thought the tournament might be cancelled because of the Covid-19 pandemic.

"I was following what was going on with Covid online," he said. "And I didn't have a good feeling about it."

The team had a scheduled workout at 4 p.m. the day before the tournament. But around 3:30, the UNK wrestlers were called to one of the rooms in the team's hotel.

"Dalton Jensen stood up in front of us and started telling everybody that the tournament had been cancelled by the NCAA," Malcom said. "It got real quiet after that. It was like a moment of silence. We had trained all year for this moment and then we were being told that we couldn't wrestle.

"It was quiet for a while before Coach McCann finally broke the silence. He told everyone how proud he was of us."

Malcom and his teammates were trying to process everything and make sense of what had just occurred.

"Everyone was experiencing so many different

emotions at that point – anger, frustration, disappointment," he said. "It was a rough experience and nobody wanted to talk about it. We were like 'what now?' I felt really bad for one of my best friends, Jarrod Hinrichs. He had placed second at nationals the year before, but then he didn't get to wrestle in the tournament as a senior. That was really tough for him."

Malcom and Hinrichs were among five Loper wrestlers who were awarded All-American honors in 2020 based on where they were seeded for the national tournament.

"We were all hoping we would get that year back," Malcom said. "But all of those seniors were done. It was really unfortunate."

Malcom came back in 2021 with hopes of winning his second national title for the Lopers. But he endured a major setback after returning home from the regional tournament. He had contracted Covid. It was less than two weeks before nationals.

"I was really sick – I was miserable," Malcom said. "I isolated for a week in my apartment. I basically just laid on the couch for almost seven days. It was really rough."

Malcom took a Covid test shortly before heading to nationals in St. Louis.

"It was barely positive," he said. "I was terrified I wasn't going to pass the test when we got down there. I had mentally prepared myself for that, but I also tried to have faith that I would pass it."

Malcom arrived in St. Louis and was tested for

Covid.

"I passed the test on Wednesday evening," he said. "I was so relieved. I had put in a lot of work for that tournament and I almost missed it."

Malcom took the mat on Friday and won his first two matches at nationals.

"I felt pretty crappy," he said. "Those first two matches were rough."

Malcom went back to the hotel and got some much-needed rest. He woke up the next morning feeling considerably better. His semifinal against Fred Green of Colorado Mesa turned out to be one of the best matches of the tournament.

"I felt really good that day and it was a barnburner of a match," Malcom said. "He ended up beating me 13-10. Losing is never fun, but that was a fun match. There were a lot of lead changes and it was a great match against a tough wrestler."

Malcom ended up placing fifth as the Lopers finished a close second to St. Cloud State in the team race.

"I didn't come back from that loss to Green very well, physically or mentally. I lost to a wrestler from St. Cloud in the consolation semifinals," Malcom said. "I didn't wrestle very well. We had pretty high hopes to win the team title, but we came up short."

Malcom was among a handful of UNK seniors who had been granted an extra year of eligibility by the NCAA because of the Covid year. And now they had to decide whether they wanted to come back or not.

"I think every single one of us seniors probably said

at one point that we were done," Malcom said. "But we all came back. I don't think there was ever a question if we would come back."

The decision paid huge dividends. Malcom won his second national title while helping lead Nebraska-Kearney to the 2022 NCAA DII team title in St. Louis.

The top-seeded Malcom won the championship at 165 pounds. He beat No. 2 seed Shane Gantz of UW-Parkside 1-0 in the finals. And Malcom became Nebraska-Kearney's first five-time All-American.

"It was an incredible season," Malcom said. "It was a total team effort. Everyone wrestled well the entire tournament. It was a great way to finish. It was so much more fun to win it again as an individual while also winning it as a team."

Malcom has stayed involved in the sport as a high school coach in Nebraska.

Malcom, who met his wife, Lily, at UNK, has fond memories of his college days.

"I truly believe I would not be the person I am without the experience I had at UNK," he said. "My coaches, my teammates and all the great people I came across during my time there really molded me into who I am. I owe all those people a lot –

"I couldn't be more thankful. I really enjoyed my time at Nebraska-Kearney. It was an awesome experience."

UNK/KEARNEY STATE ALL-AMERICANS

1975
Keven Anderson 118 6th

1978
Lane Kinnan 158 6th

1979
Tom Kruger Hwt. 6th

1980
Lane Kinnan 158 4th

Jed Dobberstein 126 8th

Walt Maslen 134 8th

Jerry Prusha 167 6th

1981
Jerry Prusha 177 6th

1982
Scott Stansbury 126 5th

Tim Vogel 158 5th

Chris Bachman 190 8th

Ted Reehl Hwt. 8th

1983
Dean Reicks Hwt. 8th

1984
Ted Reehl Hwt. 2nd

Greg Rojas 150 8th

1985
Rod Tickle Hwt. 6th

1986
Dean Reicks Hwt. 4th

Dennis Oliver 126 7th

LOPER LEGACY

1987

Dean Reicks Hwt. 2nd

Steve Roberts 158 4th

1989

Brian Hagan 118 5th

1990

Brian Hagan 118 1st

Ali Amiri-Eliasi 150 1st

1991

Ali Amiri-Eliasi 150 1st

1992

Ali Amiri-Eliasi 150 2nd

John Welsh Hwt. 3rd

Chris Guillot 118 4th

1993

Ali Amiri Eliasi 150 3rd

Shannon Peters 167 3rd

Martin Segovia 134 5th

1994

Martin Segovia 134 2nd

Jason Christiansen 142 6th

Bjorn Tomsen Hwt. 7th

1995

Martin Segovia 134 2nd

Andy McNeff 190 2nd

Bjorn Tomsen Hwt. 6th

1996

Mark Blaschko 158 8th

1997

Mark Hodgson 150 7th

1998

Joe Renfro 142 4th

Kurt Karjalainen 134 5th

Brandon Terry 167 5th

Mark Blaschko 158 6th

2000

Kurt Karjalainen 141 2nd

Brandon Pfizenmaier 149 5th

Chad Flores 133 6th

Ty Swarm 184 6th

Zach Gressett 125 7th

2001

Justin Willuweit 157 5th

Andy Sistek 197 7th

2002

Brandon Pfizenmaier 149 3rd

Bryce Abbey 125 4th

Riley Ross 165 5th

Frank Kuchera 174 5th

2003

Frank Kuchera 174 1st

Brandon Pfizenmaier 149 2nd

Bryce Abbey 125 3rd

Adam Keiswetter 133 7th

Riley Ross 165 7th

Jeff Sylvester 197 7th

2004

Jeff Sylvester 197 1st

Bryce Abbey 125 3rd

Adam Keiswetter 133 5th

2005

Adam Keiswetter 133 3rd

Bryce Abbey 125 5th

Tervel Dlagnev Hwt. 6th

Jeff Sylvester 197 7th

2006

Brett Allgood 133 1st

Tanner Linsacum 184 1st

Tervel Dlagnev Hwt. 2nd

Jeff Sylvester 197 3rd

Trevor Charbonneau 125 5th

Jeff Rutledge 141 5th

LOPER LEGACY

2007

Trevor Charbonneau 125 1st

Tervel Dlagnev Hwt. 1st

Brett Allgood 133 3rd

Joe Ellenberger 157 3rd

Jeff Rutledge 141 5th

Matt Farrell 184 5th

Taylor May 165 8th

Kelsey Empting 197 8th

2008

Brett Allgood 133 1st

Tervel Dlagnev Hwt. 1st

Jeff Rutledge 141 3rd

Ryan Etherton 149 3rd

Joe Ellenberger 157 3rd

Kamaru Usman 174 3rd

Keenan McCurdy 165 8th

Derek Ross 197 8th

2009

Kamaru Usman 174 2nd

Matt Farrell 197 3rd

Taylor May 165 5th

Joey Morrison 133 7th

Ryan Etherton 149 8th

Keenan McCurdy 157 8th

2010

Kamaru Usman 174 1st

T.J. Hepburn 157 3rd

Derek Ross 184 3rd

Taylor May 165 6th

Justin McKain 197 6th

2011

Dalton Jensen 141 2nd

T.J. Hepburn 149 2nd

Joey Wilson 165 4th

Ross Brunkhardt 184 5th

2012

Dalton Jensen 141 1st

Raufeon Stots 149 1st

T.J. Hepburn 157 1st

Joey Wilson 165 4th

Ross Brunkhardt 184 3rd

Kevin Barrett Hwt. 4th

Mark Fiala 174 8th

2013

Daniel DeShazer 133 1st

Raufeon Stots 149 1st

Chase Nelson 165 2nd

Romero Cotton 197 2nd

Brock Coutu 141 3rd

Chase White 157 5th

Patrick Martinez 174 5th

2014

Romero Cotton 197 1st

Daniel DeShazer 133 2nd

Brock Smith 165 6th

Mark Fiala 184 7th

2015

Daniel DeShazer 133 1st

Romero Cotton 197 1st

Destin McCauley 149 3rd

Devin Aguirre 165 4th

Keith Surber 141 5th

2016

Destin McCauley 149 1st

Romero Cotton 197 1st

Daniel DeShazer 133 3rd

Calvin Ochs 174 4th

Keith Surber 141 8th

2017

Keith Surber 149 1st

Destin McCauley 157 2nd

Calvin Ochs 165 4th

Zach Stodden 184 7th

2018

Matt Malcom 157 4th

Josh Portillo 125 5th

Bryce Shoemaker 133 5th

Zach Stodden 174 8th

Jarrod Hinrichs Hwt. 8th

2019

Matt Malcom 157 1st

Wesley Dawkins 133 2nd

Josh Portillo 125 2nd

Jarrod Hinrichs Hwt. 2nd

2020

Josh Portillo 125 AA

Wesley Dawkins 133 AA

Sam Turner 149 AA

Matt Malcom 165 AA

Jarrod Hinrichs Hwt. AA

2021

Wesley Dawkins 133 4th

Austin Eldredge 184 4th

Joseph Reimers 197 4th

Lee Herrington Hwt. 4th

Matt Malcom 165 5th

Nick James 141 7th

Jacob Wasser 157 7th

Terrell Garraway 174 7th

2022

Matt Malcom 165 1st

Josh Portillo 125 2nd

Wesley Dawkins 133 3rd

Billy Higgins 184 3rd

Austin Eldredge 174 4th

Nick James 141 5th

Lee Herrington Hwt. 5th

2023

Austin Eldredge 174 1st

Billy Higgins 184 6th

Lee Herrington Hwt. 7th

2024
Nick James 141 2nd

Billy Higgins 184 3rd

Crew Howard Hwt. 3rd

Jackson Kinsella 197 4th

Zach Ourada 125 5th